BBQ FOR ALL

BBQ FOR ALL

YEAR-ROUND OUTDOOR COOKING FOR VEGETARIANS, VEGANS, PESCATARIANS & MEAT-EATERS

MARCUS BAWDON

CICO BOOKS

LONDON NEW YORK

Designer Geoff Borin
Food Photography & Styling Marcus Bawdon
Editor Kate Reeves-Brown
Editorial Director Julia Charles
Head of Production Patricia Harrington
Art Director Sally Powell
Creative Director Leslie Harrington
Indexer Vanessa Bird

Published in 2023 by Dog 'n' Bone Books

An imprint of Ryland Peters & Small Ltd

20–21 Jockey's Fields   341 E 116th St,
London WC1R 4BW   New York NY 10029

www.rylandpeters.com

10 9 8 7 6 5 4 3 2

Printed and bound in China.

Notes

• Both metric and imperial/US cups are included. Work with
one set of measurements only and do not alternate between
the two within a recipe. All spoon measurements given are
level: 1 teaspoon/tsp = 5 ml; 1 tablespoon/tbsp = 15 ml.

• **FOOD SAFETY** Keep raw meat, poultry, fish and their juices
away from other food. After cutting raw meats, wash cutting
boards, utensils and countertops with hot, soapy water. Cutting
boards, utensils and countertops can be sanitized by using a
solution of 1 tbsp of unscented, liquid chlorine bleach in
4.5 litres/1 gallon of water.

• **TAKE CARE** Whenever you are cooking with live fire,
remember that any nearby surfaces will get hot, sparks can fly,
and hot liquid and fat may spill onto your skin. Always have a
first-aid kit, as well as a fire extinguisher and fire blanket, close
to where you are cooking. Always supervise children near a
barbecue or fire.

CONTENTS

INTRODUCTION

For me, everything tastes better cooked outdoors over fire...

Cooking outdoors shouldn't always be about huge slabs of meat. There is a really wonderful variety of tasty food that can be cooked over fire, all of which tastes the better for it. For me, barbecue and cooking outdoors should be tempting and exciting, whatever your food choices.

More and more people are choosing meat-free and plant-based lifestyles, and this book is an inspiration for you to pull together a real feast that will allow you to feel confident in wowing your friends and family, whatever their dietary needs.

All too often at barbecues, if anyone has any dietary requirements they end up with a pretty poor choice of foods, and there is often a real lack of imagination. Here I want to open the doors to what is possible and help you along your barbecue journey.

Here you will find a selection of meat, seafood, vegetarian and vegan options, with suitable alternatives and replacements, all equally delicious.

Barbecue has really taken off around the globe, and I'm keen for as many people as possible to discover how good food can really be when cooked over fire. On the pages that follow, I'll be giving techniques and inspiration to help you step up your outdoor cooking.

I'm hugely inspired by fire cooking techniques and food from around the globe and have been fortunate enough to have travelled and experienced many of these cooking methods first hand. I shared many of these in my previous books *Food and Fire* and *Skewered*, but there are still plenty more ideas to help you raise the bar further – and this book is full of them. Barbecue is a real journey for all involved, so enjoy the ride and you'll pick-up some new skills along the way.

Barbecue techniques

Learning to barbecue is something anyone can achieve, but there is always something new to try whatever your skill level, so be open to new techniques and ideas to expand your outdoor cooking repertoire. However, as you'll discover below, the basics of fire/heat control are very simple.

One thing that has changed over the last few years since my *Food and Fire* book, is how I teach the essential skills of heat control. I now use the most simple and effective analogy to make understanding heat control in a barbecue something anyone can achieve, no matter what type of barbecue.

Car analogy...

Barbecues come in all shapes and sizes, just like cars, and we can choose what barbecue is right for us by thinking in the same way as when we choose a car.

First is budget. It's no point looking at the most expensive of grills if our budget is more modest. How much space do you need? Do you have big parties with lots of family and friends? Or do you entertain on a smaller scale? If you cook year-round and regularly smoke big chunks of meat, you might want something insulated and more efficient. Or do you prefer something racy?

The great thing is there are grills to suit everyone, just the same as cars, whether you want something for a daily commute or just for pootling around on a Sunday.

For most people who are getting started on their journey into cooking with charcoal, a 57-cm/22-in. kettle barbecue is a good first purchase. You can do so much with one – and it's very efficient and easy to learn on, making it a perfect starter barbecue.

Then you move up to a barbecue with a bit more space. A traditional Japanese grill called a kamado is great for using all year-round and cooking for a crowd.

There are very clever barbecues that control the temperature from an app to make barbecuing easy.

There are also open grills and firepits, where you cook over the embers of a wood fire and which requires a higher skillset. Offset smokers that run on wood are renowned for cooking great food, but need constant attention.

What fuel to use?

I mostly use best-quality lumpwood charcoal to cook with. Use the best quality you can afford. Also, I love to cook over the embers of hardwoods, such as beech, oak, ash and silver birch, or fruitwoods, such as cherry (my favourite) or apple.

Those are my preferences, but feel free to cook on a grill that works for you – wonderfully tasty food can be cooked on gas or with wood-pellet grills.

Lighting the barbecue

There are three main ways to light a charcoal barbecue: using a natural wood wool firelighter; a chimney starter; or an electric charcoal starter.

Please don't use instant light charcoal, disposable barbecues (shudder), lighting gels or petroleum-based lighting products, as they will all taint the taste of your food.

Heat control

The car analogy continues... Like driving, you can control the temperature of a barbecue in the same way as you can control the speed of a car. You essentially have a brake and an accelerator pedal.

Firstly, I'd like you to think how much fuel (charcoal) you will need for the duration of your cook. Usually a couple of big handfuls of best-quality lumpwood charcoal is enough for all but the very longest of cooks.

I usually work on having coals banked up to one side and covering around one-third of the base of the grill, with no coals on the other two-thirds of the grill area. This is called two-zone cooking, and gives you a direct side over the coals and an indirect side with no coals underneath. This is the simplest and most controllable way to cook on a grill.

Like driving, you have put the right amount of fuel in for your journey (or cook). When you're ready to set off (start cooking) you need to light your coals. How many of the coals are lit will give you the first level of control on the temperature of your grill.

If half of the total coals in the two-zone setup are lit, this will give you a temperature of approximately 180–200°C/356–392°F when the lid is on. Lighting one-quarter to one-third of the coals will give you a temperature of approximately 140–160°C/284–320°F. You will surprise yourself with just how little lit charcoal you need to give you a good cooking temperature when the lid is on, and just how long the coals will last.

Once the coals are lit and the lid is on, you get to tweak the barbecue temperature in the same way as driving your car. The vent on top of any lidded barbecue acts as a brake, trapping combustion gases and smoke when closed and slowing the coals down. The air inlet at the base of the barbecue acts as an accelerator pedal – the more air that can get to the coals, the hotter they become.

When I drive my car I speed-up slowly with the accelerator and then ease off as I get to the speed I want, using the brake only if I have to. I control the temperature of my barbecue in the same way, opening the air inlet until almost at the temperature I want, then gradually shutting it until just a small opening is left. Every barbecue is different, but using this technique will help you get a better feel for controlling the heat.

So when do you use the brake? At the end of the journey or if you feel out of control – maybe the wind picks up or some fat starts flaring up – if the air inlet is hardly open, a little brake applied (around half way closed) will help you get back in control. This technique obviously only works for barbecues with a lid.

In an open grill or firepit you can't control the airflow, so the amount of wood or charcoal added to the fire becomes the accelerator pedal.

This simple technique of barbecue heat control has helped many thousands of people understand what is going on when they adjust the vents on their barbecue. Try it.

Adding smoke

On all forms of barbecuing, from gas to charcoal, you can add an element of smoke to your food. This can often be a wonderful thing, but please bear in mind to use fruitwoods, hardwoods and nutwoods only. Go gently; one or two chunks or a small handful of chips is enough.

Hardwoods such as oak can be overpowering if used too much. Some people are more sensitive to smoke and can find it too much. Sometimes smoke can clash with other flavours, so be careful. I always add a chunk of cherry wood to whatever I'm smoking; I love the colour and sweet smoke it brings to the party. Mesquite… just no. Less is almost always more. Think subtle smoke for best flavour.

A word about flavour

I see flavours in cooking – not just barbecuing – as achieving balance. It's vital to avoid having one flavour overpowering the rest. You want them working together in harmony, and this is even more important in barbecued food.

Imagine a musical orchestra… it has its different sections of wind, strings and percussion. When they are all in harmony, the music is beautiful. If the drums are out of time, or the trombone is flat, that is all you will hear. If your barbecue food is out of balance, too sweet, smoky or salty, then it will throw everything out flavour-wise. A balanced flavour approach is worth striving for, so taste everything.

What other equipment do I need?

You don't need a huge amount of specialized kit, but the following things I see as pretty important in helping you on your barbecue journey:

• A good butchers' boning knife and a chefs' knife.

• A couple of good thermometers; an instant-read probe thermometer and a thermometer you can leave in the food with the barbecue lid on, such as a wired probe, or wireless probe such as Meater®.

• Some solid heatproof tongs and a spatula.

• A charcoal chimney starter.

• Heatproof welding gloves.

This will be enough to get you started, although once you get into barbecuing, you'll find all sorts of kit you suddenly need or want!

TIPS FOR MEAT

The quality of the meat you buy will have a real impact on how your food turns out. I don't insist you buy the most expensive organic and free-range meat, however, if you buy the best-quality meat you can afford, then your barbecuing will be the better for it. Good-quality, but cheaper, fattier cuts are often more affordable, and these are at their best when barbecued low and slow to break down the collagen.

Getting the right sort of heat for the cut of meat you are cooking is imperative. You need low heat and indirect grilling for those tough, collagen-rich cuts, such as ribs and brisket (we call this low and slow cooking). However, for searing steaks, you'll need a higher direct heat.

One of the best tips I can give you for cooking meat is to invest in a good-quality digital meat thermometer or two, ideally a probe type or a leave-in type. This will give you confidence and accuracy in your meat cooking to know that it's cooked safely and to your preferred doneness; without a thermometer you are really just guessing.

I generally like to take my meat out of the fridge for a while before cooking, so that it's not fridge-cold, especially when roasting joints such as beef and lamb. This will stop the outside of the meat overcooking before the core of the meat gets up to temperature. However, thin steaks can be cooked straight from the fridge, so you can get a good sear on the outside without overcooking the inside. Low-and-slow cuts, such as brisket, come straight from the fridge and onto the smoker, as you get a better smoke flavour into the meat when it's still cold.

Seasoning meat is really important. Getting the right amount of salt on a steak gives you a good balance of flavour; under-seasoning will give a bland result and over-seasoning will affect the flavour of the meat. Seasoning is a very personal thing, as we all have differing tastes, but my general advice is to go bold, and to give the meat a shake to remove any excess seasoning. Be careful with pepper and spices

when cooking over direct heat as they can burn and taste bitter.

Resting meat is a critical part of the process, as when you take meat off a hot grill, it will carry on increasing in temperature. If you are searing or roasting meats, you can monitor this with a meat thermometer by taking the meat off the barbecue around 5°C/40°F before it reaches the preferred temperature, then rest it until the internal temperature stops going up. If you are smoking meats low and slow, a long rest will keep the meat juicier. I like to serve my low and slow cuts, such as brisket, at around 70°C/158°F once they have rested and cooled.

Finally, always cut your meat across the grain where possible.

TIPS FOR VEG

Cooking vegetables on the barbecue makes them really come alive – the searing heat and char allow the sugars to caramelize and develop the best flavour. Fresher veg will always taste better than any that have been sitting around for a while.

Where veg has a skin, you can allow this to get really charred, protecting the veg inside. Onions, (bell) peppers and aubergines (eggplants) have natural wrappers.

A light coating of olive oil will stop veg drying out when grilling. Bastes and marinades work really well with grilled veg, but be careful with oil-based marinades and bastes, as the oil will drip onto the coals and flare up. Subtle seasonings work best, so they are not overpowering the flavours.

Use a probe thermometer or skewer to test veg for softness in the middle – there should be hardly any resistance when probed.

Getting the heat right is really important, as is getting the veg close to the direct heat source (i.e., the charcoal). If the veg is too far away from the charcoal, you won't get any of the magic of caramelization, and the veg will just dry out and become leathery.

A plate of simply grilled veg with a flavourful dressing such as chimichurri is a real revelation. Experiment with flavours and bring new life to veg on the barbecue!

TIPS FOR FISH

One of the most common things I get asked in my UK BBQ School classes is how to cook fish on a barbecue. It seems this is one of the things people struggle with the most, even once they have got the hang of temperature control.

The main tip I can give you is to use the freshest fish you can get hold of. This really does make all the difference.

Dry the fish skin with paper towels before rubbing in a little oil and seasoning. Don't overdo the seasoning, but, just like with meat, you want to get that balance just right.

A nice clean but seasoned grill is vital if you want to avoid the fish sticking to the grill. Take your grill grate off the barbecue before lighting, so you are placing your fish on a cold grate.

Use something in-between the fish and the grill grates to stop it sticking. This could be slices of lemon, a sheet of foil, a cedar plank, some herbs or some opened-out leeks.

Finally, another great idea is to suspend your fish on skewers over the coals, so that the fish doesn't touch the grill. This is a game changer when it comes to cooking delicate fish. Go on, try it!

CHAPTER 1

VEG

EMBER-COOKED BABA GANOUSH

Aubergines/eggplants are just made for cooking direct in the embers; their taste and texture totally transform. The soft flesh makes the most wonderful dip for a few crackers or crisp flatbreads. Like all the best things, it is simple and delicious.

Set up your barbecue for direct cooking in the coals at a moderate heat (around 160°C/320°F). Use best-quality lumpwood charcoal or hardwood/fruitwood embers. You can also use a firepit.

Pierce the aubergine/eggplant skin with a knife tip in a couple of places, then place them onto the coals. Cook for a few minutes to char the skin, turning every so often until the skin is charred and the inside flesh soft, around 10–12 minutes.

Place on a plate and allow to cool for 5 minutes, then cut a slice along one side of the aubergine/eggplant and use a spoon to loosen the soft, stringy flesh without damaging the skin.

Gently combine the tahini, garlic, lemon juice, olive oil and cumin with the flesh to form a rich paste. Season with a pinch of sea salt and black pepper, then sprinkle over the chilli flakes/hot red pepper flakes and flat-leaf parsley. Serve.

1 large aubergine/eggplant

2 tbsp tahini

1 clove garlic, crushed

freshly squeezed juice of ½ lemon

1 tbsp extra virgin olive oil

1 tsp cumin powder

1 tsp Aleppo chilli flakes/hot red pepper flakes

1 tbsp freshly chopped flat-leaf parsley

coarse sea salt and freshly ground black pepper

Serves 2

AUBERGINE/EGGPLANT BRUSCHETTA

One of my younger brothers is a very health-conscious vegan, and he recently came to visit us with his family. I love to set myself culinary challenges, so I wanted to give him a couple of dishes that he, and my family of fully committed carnivores, would both enjoy. This aubergine/eggplant bruschetta is a simple tasty treat that went down well. It makes a great little appetizer.

150 g/5¼ oz. semi-dried tomatoes in oil

2 aubergines/eggplants, sliced into 1-cm/½-in. thick rounds

2 tbsp dried oregano

200 g/7 oz. feta, mozzarella or vegan cheese, crumbled or torn

a handful of sliced olives (optional)

coarse sea salt and freshly ground black pepper

baking sheet, lined with foil

Serves 4

Set up your barbecue for lid-on indirect cooking at a high heat (around 180–200°C/356–392°F). You can also use a wood-fired oven.

Drain the tomatoes, reserving the oil.

Top the aubergine/eggplant slices with the tomatoes. Sprinkle with the oregano and top with the cheese of your choice and some olives, if you like. Drizzle a little of the reserved oil from the tomatoes over the top and season with salt and pepper.

Place on the foil-lined baking sheet and place into the barbecue for about 20 minutes until the aubergine/eggplant is softened and the cheese melted and slightly browned. Serve at once.

GARLIC MUSHROOM TOASTS

You don't always need a big meal – sometimes a delicious something on toast works a treat. You can whip something together for a quick midweek tea using just a handful of lit charcoal and some fresh ingredients. I saw this special selection of mushrooms, and wanted to make the most to celebrate them. Toasting the bread directly on the coals provides a delicious lightly charred throne for them to be transported to your waiting mouth.

15 g/1 tbsp salted butter

250 g/9 oz. mixed mushrooms

1 clove garlic, finely chopped

2 tbsp freshly chopped flat-leaf parsley

4 slices ciabatta or sourdough bread

coarse sea salt and freshly ground black pepper

cast-iron or heavy-duty pan

Serves 2

Set up your barbecue for direct cooking at a moderate heat (around 160–180°C/320–356°F).

Place the cast-iron pan over the direct heat, add the butter and allow to melt until it starts to froth. Pop the mushrooms in the pan and cook for a few minutes, then add the finely chopped garlic and season with a pinch of salt and pepper.

Cook until the mushrooms are lightly browned and softened. Sprinkle the parsley over the top of the mushrooms and remove from the heat.

Toast the bread on both sides over the coals, then place onto plates. Top the toast with the mushrooms and any juices from the pan. Serve at once.

DIRTY PEPPER TOASTS

At my UK BBQ School classes I try to be as inclusive as possible of all diets, so I'm always looking for simple vegetarian alternatives to some of my meat recipes. These dirty pepper toasts are just as tasty as dirty steak sandwiches (see page 124) and the smell of the sweet charred peppers on the coals gets everyone's mouths watering.

Set up your barbecue for direct cooking in the coals at a moderate heat (around 160–180°C/320–356°F). Use best-quality lumpwood charcoal or hardwood/fruitwood embers. You can also use a firepit.

Place the peppers directly onto the coals and cook for 5–6 minutes until blackened and softened, turning as needed. Set them aside to continue softening.

Make up the herb sauce by popping the oregano, garlic, olive oil, red wine vinegar and a pinch of salt and pepper into a blender or food processor and blitz until you get a coarse, herby sauce. You can also use a mortar and pestle.

Toast the bread either directly on or over the coals on both sides. Put the toast on plates and brush with a little of the herb sauce.

Remove as much of the charred skin of the peppers as you like (a little left on adds to the flavour). Slice the peppers into thin rings and place onto the toasted bread slices. Drizzle the rest of the herby sauce on top and serve at once.

2 sweet pointed red (bell) peppers

2 tbsp freshly chopped oregano

1 small clove garlic

4 tbsp extra virgin olive oil

1 tsp red wine vinegar

4 pieces focaccia or sourdough bread

coarse sea salt and freshly ground black pepper

Serves 2

KIMCHEESE QUESADILLA

This is one of those delicious little snacky things which, with a few salads or side dishes, can make a filling lunch. It is also great to knock up quickly when you need to put something together at the last minute. Kimchi (a Korean dish of salted and fermented vegetables) is readily available these days, and here the tangy kimchi, melty oozy cheese and crisp flour tortilla work so well together.

4 mini flour tortillas

4 tbsp kimchi

a small handful of grated Cheddar cheese

a small handful of grated mozzarella cheese

2 spring onions/scallions, thinly sliced

cast-iron or heavy-duty pan or plancha (optional)

Serves 2

Set up your barbecue for direct cooking at a low–moderate heat (around 140–160°C/284–320°F) or place a cast-iron pan or plancha over moderate direct heat.

Place a flour tortilla directly onto the grill or in the cast-iron pan. Add 2 tbsp kimchi and a good sprinkle each of grated Cheddar and mozzarella, then place another tortilla on top.

Cook for a few minutes on each side until the tortilla is toasted and crisp, and the cheese is melted and gooey. Remove from the heat and repeat with the remaining ingredients to make a second quesadilla.

Slice each quesadilla in half and top with the sliced spring onions/scallions. Serve at once.

GRILLED SWEETHEART CABBAGE TOPPED WITH SPICED BUTTER AND ALMONDS

This recipe is so tasty and works wonderfully as an appetizer, but it makes a great side dish, too, perhaps with some naan and a good dhal. The key is to get some nice crispy charred edges and for the cabbage to soften as you baste it with the delicious spiced butter. For a vegan alternative simply swap the butter for an additional 4–5 tbsp rapeseed oil.

2 tbsp flaked/sliced almonds

1 sweetheart cabbage

1 tbsp rapeseed oil

50 g/3½ tbsp softened salted butter

1 tsp Kashmiri or tandoori masala powder

1 tsp turmeric powder

1 tsp cumin powder

1 tsp Aleppo chilli flakes/hot red pepper flakes

coarse sea salt and freshly ground black pepper

small cast-iron or heavy-duty pan

Serves 2

Set up your barbecue for lid-on direct cooking at a moderate heat (around 160–180°C/320–356°F).

Lightly toast the flaked/sliced almonds in the small pan over the coals and set aside. Coarsely chop the almonds once cool.

Cut the sweetheart cabbage in half lengthways, brush it lightly with the rapeseed oil and season lightly, then place on the grill. Cook for around 10–15 minutes until the edges of the cabbage are charred.

While the cabbage is cooking, make a spiced butter to baste over it. Mix together the softened butter, Kashmiri or tandoori masala powder, turmeric and cumin, and stir until combined.

Once the cabbage is nicely charred, start to brush the spiced butter onto the cut side of the cabbage with a pastry or silicon brush. Continue to cook for 5–6 minutes, brushing with the butter every couple of minutes. You should see the cabbage start to soften.

Sprinkle with the chilli flakes/hot red pepper flakes and chopped toasted almonds and lightly season to taste. Serve at once.

YAKI ONIGIRI

Yaki onigiri (Japanese grilled rice balls) are simple and delicious when grilled over good charcoal. Here, my recipe is cooked on a traditional Japanese konro grill, using some very special binchotan charcoal, but you can cook these on any grill at home.

500 g/generous 2⅔ cups sushi rice

650 ml/2¾ cups water

4 tbsp light soy sauce

4 tbsp mirin

1 sheet wakame seaweed, crumbled

Sriracha mayo, to drizzle

Serves 4

Set up your barbecue for direct cooking at a moderate heat (around 160–180°C/320–356°F).

Rinse the sushi rice in a sieve/strainer under the cold tap/faucet to remove excess starch, then allow to drain completely.

Place the rice in a pan with a lid and add 650 ml/2¾ cups water. Bring to the boil on the hob/stovetop, then turn the heat down to low and simmer with the lid on for 15 minutes. Turn off the heat and leave with the lid on for 10 minutes.

Transfer the rice to a large flat plate and spread it out to cool.

Mix together the soy sauce and mirin. Set aside.

Once cool, divide the rice into four portions and shape each portion with wet hands into a flattened oval.

Grill the rice shapes over direct heat until the surface of the rice begins to crisp up, turning them carefully every couple of minutes. Glaze with the soy sauce and mirin using a silicon or pastry brush.

Top with some crumbled wakame seaweed and a drizzle of Sriracha mayo and serve. Delicious.

CHARRED LEEK RAFTS

This is a wonderful vegetarian alternative to the sausage rafts that were in my book Skewered. *They are equally delicious with the charred leeks smothered with melted Cheddar cheese and chimichurri. A truly delicious combination.*

6 leeks

1 tsp extra virgin olive oil

a handful of grated mature/ sharp Cheddar cheese or vegan cheese

coarse sea salt and freshly ground black pepper

CHIMICHURRI

2 cloves garlic

a handful of flat-leaf parsley and oregano

1 tbsp dried oregano

a pinch of smoked paprika

60 ml/4 tbsp extra virgin olive oil

2 tbsp red wine vinegar

1 tbsp Aleppo chilli flakes/hot red pepper flakes

2 wooden skewers, soaked in water

Serves 2

Set up your barbecue for lid-on direct cooking at a moderate heat (around 160–180°C/320–356°F).

Trim the leeks, then place them next to each other and use the soaked wooden skewers to make a raft with the leeks, skewering through the leeks close to either end to make a raft.

Rub the olive oil over the leeks, lightly season with a pinch of salt and pepper and place on the grill. Cook for 8–10 minutes with the lid on until the outside of the leeks has charred slightly and they have softened.

While the leeks are cooking, blitz up all the chimichurri ingredients with a couple of good pinches of coarse sea salt in a food processor or blender.

Place the cheese on top of the leeks, then close the barbecue lid again and cook for a few minutes until the cheese has melted. Drizzle over a couple of teaspoons of the chimichurri and serve.

SMOKY BUTTERNUT SQUASH

By cooking a butternut squash on the barbecue until the skin becomes slightly charred, the smoky flavour works its way through the flesh. The spicy maple butter and thyme work beautifully with these charred, smoky flavours.

1 butternut squash

60 g/4 tbsp softened butter

2 tsp maple syrup

2 tsp Aleppo chilli flakes/hot red pepper flakes

8 sprigs of thyme

coarse sea salt and freshly ground black pepper

Serves 2

Set up your barbecue for lid-on direct cooking at a moderate heat (around 160°C/320°F).

Place the butternut squash on the grill and cook it for 40–60 minutes with the barbecue lid on, turning it every 10 minutes. It should be soft and lightly charred on the outside (if it's charring too much, move it to the indirect side).

Mix the butter, maple syrup and chilli flakes/hot red pepper flakes in a bowl until combined.

Once cooked through, place the squash on a serving plate and cut in half lengthways, removing any seeds and stringy bits.

Use a fork to mash up the soft smoky flesh, and season with salt and pepper. Spoon over the spicy maple butter to melt, sprinkle over the thyme sprigs and serve.

CHIMICHURRI ROASTIES

When running my barbecue classes at UK BBQ School, I often change my dishes around. One of my recent inclusions has proven a real hit, and so many people just can't get enough of these chimichurri roasties and ask for the recipe, so here it is! These could be a side, but just a bowl of these by themselves is a feast.

1 kg/2 lb. 4 oz. baby/new potatoes

4 tbsp extra virgin olive oil

coarse sea salt and freshly ground black pepper

CHIMICHURRI

2 cloves garlic

80 ml/⅓ cup extra virgin olive oil

2 tsp red wine vinegar

2 tbsp dried oregano

2 tbsp Aleppo chilli flakes/hot red pepper flakes

a small handful of oregano or marjoram

a good handful of flat-leaf parsley

heavy-duty roasting pan

Serves 4

Parboil the potatoes for around 10 minutes until soft (check with the point of a sharp knife). Drain the potatoes.

Blitz up all the chimichurri ingredients with a couple of good pinches of coarse sea salt in a food processor or blender.

Set up your barbecue for direct cooking at a moderate heat (around 160–180°C/320–356°F). You can also cook the roasties in an open fire grill, firepit or wood-fired oven.

Place the potatoes in the heavy-duty roasting pan, drizzle over the olive oil and season with a good pinch of coarse sea salt and black pepper.

Place the roasting pan on the barbecue directly over the coals. The roasties will start to crisp up after 20–30 minutes, depending on the exact temperature of your coals.

Once the potatoes are nicely crisp and maybe a little charred in places, spoon over the chimichurri and serve hot.

CHEESE-AND-ONION-TOPPED HASSELBACK POTATOES

My kids are always asking for hasselback potatoes these days; they love the crispy outside texture and soft insides when you cook them on the barbecue. I'm always looking for different toppings to make them a bit more fun. The melted cheese and crispy onion topping went down very well, with the cheese oozing into the gaps between the potato slices.

8 potatoes, all a similar size

2 tbsp olive oil

200 g/2 cups grated melting cheese, such as Cheddar or mozzarella

4 tbsp crispy onion flakes

coarse sea salt and freshly ground black pepper

Serves 4

Set up your barbecue for lid-on indirect cooking at a high heat (around 200°C/392°F). You can also use a wood-fired oven.

Place two wooden spoons on a chopping board and place a potato in-between the handles. Using a sharp knife, cut down into the potato, using the spoon handles to stop you cutting all the way through. Continue slicing every 3 mm/⅛ in. to create the hasselback effect. Repeat for all of the potatoes.

Drizzle the potatoes with the olive oil and rub it in. Season generously with sea salt and black pepper.

Place the potatoes on the barbecue and cook them over indirect heat with the lid on for around 40 minutes until the outside is crispy and the potatoes are cooked through.

Sprinkle the cheese on top followed by the crispy onion flakes, then cook with the lid on for a further 5 minutes until the cheese has melted.

SMOKY CELERIAC/CELERY ROOT DAUPHINOISE

I've been reducing the amount of carbs I've been eating for the last couple of years, and this recipe has been one of my favourite things to make. Personally I think it is even tastier with celeriac/celery root than potato, and even better with a touch of smoke.

Set up your barbecue for lid-on indirect cooking at a moderate heat (around 160°C/320°F), with a chunk of light smoking wood, such as cherry wood, on the coals.

Remove the skin from the celeriac/celery root with a peeler or sharp knife and remove any parts of the root. Cut the celeriac/celery root in half from the top through the middle, then slice it into thin half-moon slices (as thin as you can get with a very sharp knife).

Lay the sliced celeriac/celery root in the pan, sprinkle over the finely chopped garlic and pour over the cream and milk. Add the butter to the top and season with a good pinch of salt and pepper.

Place on the barbecue and cook over indirect heat with the lid on for about 40 minutes until cooked through, ensuring the pan doesn't burn or run dry. The celeriac/celery root should be nice and soft, the creamy sauce reduced and the top lovely and brown.

1 celeriac/celery root

1 clove garlic, finely chopped

200 ml/scant 1 cup double/heavy cream

200 ml/scant 1 cup full-fat/whole milk

15 g/1 tbsp butter

coarse sea salt and freshly ground black pepper

cast-iron or heavy-duty pan

Serves 2

CAULIFLOWER MUSTARD CRUMBLE

A whole cauliflower oozing with cheese and topped with a crumble of crispy cooked onions can be a real centrepiece for a feast. Cut into thick wedges, this is a real treat. I cooked mine in a wood-fired oven, but this can also be easily cooked on the indirect side of a barbecue with a lid.

2 cauliflowers

6 tbsp American mustard, plus extra to drizzle

2 tbsp rapeseed oil

500 g/generous 5 cups grated mature/sharp Cheddar cheese

2 tbsp freshly chopped flat-leaf parsley

4 tbsp crispy onions

coarse sea salt and freshly ground black pepper

Serves 8

Set up your barbecue for lid-on indirect cooking at a high heat (around 180°C/356°F). You can also use a wood-fired oven.

Remove most of the cauliflower stalks, leaving just a few leaves. Place the cauliflowers onto a baking sheet.

Mix the mustard with the oil and brush onto the cauliflowers. Cover them lightly with foil.

Cook over indirect heat with the lid on for 40 minutes, then remove the foil and cook for another 20 minutes.

Sprinkle over the grated cheese and cook for another 15–20 minutes until the cheese is browned and bubbling.

Drizzle over a little more mustard and sprinkle over the flat-leaf parsley and crispy onions. Serve cut into thick wedges.

GRILLED VEG WITH ZHOUG

Simple but bold flavours are celebrated in this dish. Zhoug (or zhug) is a wonderfully punchy spicy, coriander/cilantro-rich condiment from Yemen, similar to chimichurri (see page 33). It's delicious.

a selection of veg for grilling, such as sweet (bell) peppers, aubergine/eggplant, courgette/zucchini, onion and asparagus

1 lemon, halved

3 tbsp extra virgin olive oil

coarse sea salt and freshly ground black pepper

ZHOUG

a handful of coriander/cilantro, around 30 g/1 oz.

a small handful of flat-leaf parsley, around 20 g/¾ oz.

1 green chilli/chile

1 plump clove garlic

1 tsp cumin powder

a small pinch of cumin seeds

freshly squeezed juice of ½ lemon

1 tsp Aleppo chilli flakes/hot red pepper flakes

80 ml/⅓ cup extra virgin olive oil

Serves 4

Make up the zhoug by blitzing up all the ingredients into a fine sauce using a stick blender or crush them together using a mortar and pestle.

Set up your barbecue for direct cooking at a moderate heat (around 160–180°C/320–356°F). You could even cook the veg dirty-style directly on the charcoal.

Start off with the veg that take the longest to cook (onions, courgettes/zucchini and aubergine/eggplant) and cut them into 1-cm/½-in. thick circles. Drizzle the cut veg and the lemon halves with a little of the olive oil and season with salt and pepper. Grill them over direct heat until they begin to caramelize and soften.

Add the (bell) peppers and finally the asparagus, and continue to cook until all have a nice light charring.

Plate up the veg and drizzle over the zhoug sauce.

GRILLED VEG BUDDHA BOWL

Eating veg from the grill certainly doesn't mean missing out on taste – this dish is packed with flavour. A Buddha bowl is a selection of varied ingredients on a rice base, most often plant-based. You can, of course, tailor this to your own tastes, even adding meat or fish. I went with a delicious veggie version here. The nice thing with this is that you can grill up a good range of tasty ingredients, and then everyone can choose what they want and build their bowl.

a selection of veg for grilling, such as mini sweet (bell) peppers, spring onions/scallions, courgette/zucchini slices and sugar snap peas

2 tbsp mayonnaise

1 tsp Sriracha

freshly squeezed juice of ½ lime

500 g/3¾ cups sushi rice, cooked according to the packet instructions

a handful of salad leaves

1 large ripe avocado

1 tsp chilli flakes/hot red pepper flakes

2 tbsp freshly chopped coriander/cilantro

2 tbsp light soy sauce

Serves 2

Set up your barbecue for direct cooking at a high heat (around 180–200°C/356–392°F).

Place the veg on the grill over the coals to char slightly, around 5–6 minutes.

Meanwhile, mix together the mayonnaise, Sriracha and lime juice. Set aside.

Divide the cooked rice between two bowls and add the salad leaves. Arrange the grilled veg artfully on top. Scoop out the avocado flesh and slice it, placing half in each bowl.

Drizzle over the Sriracha lime mayo, the chilli flakes/hot red pepper flakes, coriander/cilantro and a little soy sauce. Serve.

CELERIAC/CELERY ROOT STEAKS WITH WHITE BARBECUE SAUCE

If you are yet to try a white barbecue sauce, you might be highly surprised at how good it is. The original, hailing from Alabama, is mayonnaise-based and works so well on smoky chicken. But the version I've made here goes so well with many vegetable dishes. I went for celeriac/celery root 'steaks', which are a great match for the tangy white barbecue sauce. Feel free to try other veg, such as cauliflower, with this sauce.

1 celeriac/celery root

2 tbsp olive oil

coarse sea salt and freshly ground black pepper

WHITE BARBECUE SAUCE

6 tbsp mayonnaise

1 tbsp apple cider vinegar

1 tbsp pickle juice (from a jar of pickles)

1 tbsp water

1 tsp cream of horseradish

1 tsp American mustard

1 tsp Worcestershire sauce

½ tsp garlic powder

½ tsp coarse ground black pepper

½ tsp sea salt

¼ tsp hot sauce of your choice

Serves 2

Set up your barbecue for lid-on direct cooking at a moderate heat (around 160–180°C/320–356°F).

Make up the white barbecue sauce by mixing the ingredients together until they form a rich, creamy and tangy sauce.

Remove the outer skin of the celeriac/celery root and cut it into steaks around 1 cm/½ in. thick. Pour over the olive oil and rub it into the celeriac/celery root steaks. Season with salt and pepper.

Place the celeriac/celery root steaks on the grill and cook direct, turning occasionally, for about 12–15 minutes until they have seared slightly, are a lovely caramel colour in places and have softened.

Plate up the celeriac/celery root steaks and drizzle over the white barbecue sauce. Serve at once.

KIMCHEESE CAULIFLOWER SLICES

I've been playing with my food again… I'm especially fond of veg from which you can create a 'steak' (such as cauliflower and celeriac/celery root) to be grilled and topped with all sorts of exciting flavours. The taste of charred cauliflower with the bold flavours of kimchi (see page 22) and mature Cheddar surprised me with how well it worked. And I love surprises! In this recipe I have gone with a beetroot/beet kimchi, but this will work well with any kimchi.

Set up your barbecue for lid-on two-zone (direct and indirect) grilling at a moderate heat (around 150–160°C/302–320°F).

Slice the cauliflower into four thick steaks, from the top of the cauliflower to the bottom. You'll end up with two wider steaks (from the middle of the cauliflower) and two smaller steaks (from the edges).

Rub the oil all over the cauliflower steaks and place them on the grill. Cook over direct heat for 12–15 minutes, watching that they don't burn (a little char is ok, but if they char too quickly, move them to the indirect side of the grill).

Once the cauliflower is charred and softened, spoon 2 tbsp kimchi onto each cauliflower steak, then sprinkle the grated Cheddar cheese over the top.

Pop them back onto the indirect side of the grill, and cook for another 4–5 minutes with the lid on until the cheese has melted.

1 cauliflower

2 tbsp cold-pressed rapeseed oil

8 tbsp beetroot/beet kimchi or other kimchi

100 g/1 cup grated mature/ sharp Cheddar cheese

Serves 2

GRILLED VEG FONDUE

Charred vegetable skewers dipped into a creamy cheesy fondue is a match made in heaven. A lick of cherry smoke to the cheesy dipping sauce gives it a wonderful depth of flavour. You could set this up using a small table-top grill to keep the fondue warm and to sit round to grill the veg with a few friends. Very social eating.

a selection of veg for grilling, such as sweet (bell) peppers, courgettes/zucchini, spring onions/scallions, leeks and aubergine/eggplant

2 tbsp olive oil

coarse sea salt and freshly ground black pepper

CHEESY FONDUE DIP

150 g/1½ cups grated melting cheese, such as a mix of mature/sharp Cheddar and mozzarella

300 ml/1¼ cups double/heavy cream

3 tbsp cream cheese

1 small clove garlic, sliced

1 tsp dried oregano

1 tsp hot sauce

4 wooden skewers, soaked in water

cast-iron or heavy-duty pan

Serves 4

Set up your barbecue for direct cooking at a moderate heat (around 160–180°C/320–356°F), with some indirect space for the cast-iron pan. Add a chunk of sweet cherry wood for a lovely smoky flavour.

Cut the veg into 2.5-cm/1-in. pieces and push the pieces onto the skewers. Drizzle over the olive oil and season with salt and pepper. Alternatively, cut a selection of veg suitable for grilling and let your guests make their own skewers.

Place the cast-iron pan onto the barbecue to the edge of the heat and add all of the ingredients for the dip, along with some salt and pepper. Allow to bubble and keep stirring with a spoon to ensure it doesn't burn, keeping the lid on the barbecue when you can.

Once the fondue ingredients have combined and the cheese has melted, move the pan to a cooler part of the barbecue.

Start grilling your veg skewers over direct heat, a few minutes on each side until the veg is charred on the edges and starting to soften. You can get your guests involved in doing this, and then they can dip their own skewers into the fondue.

EMBER-CHARRED RATATOUILLE

I made this dish from a selection of veg that my local farm shop couldn't sell as it was just at the point before it became overripe. I snapped it up and then really wanted to celebrate the sweet, ripe vegetables. The stars were some heritage tomatoes that were simply too good to waste. Cooking any veg directly on the embers, gives a wonderful char and caramelization, which then transfers beautifully into a stunning ratatouille. Ideally pick up some veg at the peak of its ripeness, maybe have a chat with your local greengrocer and offer to take any overripe veg off their hands. You can vary the veg according to what you have.

2 courgettes/zucchini

1 aubergine/eggplant

2 red onions, halved

1 garlic bulb

6–8 medium–large very ripe tomatoes

6–8 mushrooms

a few sweet (bell) peppers

4 tsp extra virgin olive oil, plus extra to drizzle

1 tbsp dried oregano

1 tbsp red wine vinegar

2 tbsp tomato purée/paste

a sprig of rosemary

a handful of freshly chopped flat-leaf parsley

coarse sea salt and freshly ground black pepper

cast-iron or heavy-duty pan

Serves 4

Set up your barbecue for direct cooking on coals at a moderate heat (around 160–180°C/320–356°F), with a couple of handfuls of best-quality lumpwood charcoal. Remove the grill grate and spread the coals out in an even layer. You can also use a firepit.

Place the larger veg (courgettes/zucchini, aubergine/eggplant, halved red onions and whole garlic bulb) on the coals first and cook for around 10 minutes, turning every few minutes, until charred on the outside and starting to soften. Then add the smaller veg (tomatoes, mushrooms and peppers) directly to the coals and cook for a further 8–10 minutes until everything has softened and is moderately charred on the outside.

Coarsely chop all the cooked vegetables and squeeze the garlic cloves from their skins.

Place the cast-iron pan onto the coals and pour in the olive oil. Add all of the chopped veg, the dried oregano, red wine vinegar and tomato purée/paste, and season with a couple of good pinches of coarse sea salt and black pepper.

Toast the rosemary sprig directly on the coals for a few seconds until it starts to smoke, then finely chop the leaves and add to the ratatouille. Allow the ratatouille to bubble gently in the pan for around 10 minutes, adding a splash or two of water if it starts to dry out.

Finish off with the flat-leaf parsley sprinkled over and a drizzle of good olive oil.

Perfect served with a chunk of good bread to mop up the juices.

SPANISH RICE WITH GRILLED PADRONS

Paella of sorts is a firm family favourite with my clan. It's certainly never a traditional paella, but something simpler. This recipe is vegan, but a few grilled chicken thighs and pan-fried chorizo chunks can be added separately for those who choose. Or perhaps some grilled prawns/shrimp? This versatile dish is hard to beat.

4 tbsp extra virgin olive oil

2 onions, finely chopped

2 cloves garlic, finely chopped

1 red (bell) pepper, chopped

1 yellow (bell) pepper, chopped

1 green (bell) pepper, chopped

2 tbsp smoked paprika

750 g/4 cups paella rice

a pinch of saffron, soaked in 2 tbsp hot water

3 litres/12 cups hot vegetable stock

1 lemon, cut into 8 wedges

a handful of freshly chopped flat-leaf parsley

200 g/7 oz. padron peppers

coarse sea salt and freshly ground black pepper

paella pan or large flat pan that will fit in your barbecue with the lid down

Serves 8

Set up your barbecue for lid-on direct cooking at a moderate heat (around 150°C/302°F).

Place the paella pan over the heat and add the olive oil, onions, garlic and (bell) peppers, and cook for around 10 minutes until the onions have softened and are lightly caramelized. Add the paprika and stir. Add a couple of pinches of salt and ground black pepper.

Add the paella rice and cook for 4–5 minutes to toast the grains and coat them in oil. Pour in the saffron with the soaking water, followed by 1 litre/4 cups of the hot stock. Pop the lid of the barbecue on and cook for 10 minutes until most of the stock has been absorbed.

Add another 1 litre/4 cups of stock and cook for a further 10 minutes, then add the final 1 litre/4 cups of stock and cook for around 15 minutes until all of the stock has been absorbed.

Top the rice with the lemon wedges and sprinkle over the flat-leaf parsley. Remove the pan from the heat and set aside to rest.

Grill the padron peppers directly over the coals until slightly charred, blistered and starting to soften. Place the charred padron peppers on top of the rice and serve.

CHAPTER 2

FISHY

MUSSELS IN BEER

Having some sort of heavy-duty pot with a lid to cook on a barbecue is a real bonus and opens up so many wonderful cooking opportunities. Some simply cooked mussels over a fire are one of my favourite things to eat, served in a big bowl with a chunk or two of crusty bread to dip in the juices.

15 g/1 tbsp butter

2 cloves garlic, finely chopped

1 kg/2 lb. 4 oz. live mussels, debearded

200 ml/scant 1 cup light beer, such as lager or fruity IPA

freshly squeezed juice of ½ lemon

2 tbsp freshly chopped flat-leaf parsley

coarse sea salt and freshly ground black pepper

chunks of rustic bread, such as focaccia or sourdough, to serve

cast-iron Dutch oven or heavy-duty pan with a lid

Serves 2

Set up your barbecue for direct cooking at a moderate heat (around 160°C/320°F). You can also use a firepit or wood-fired oven.

Put the cast-iron Dutch oven or pan on the barbecue to get hot, either straight in the coals or on a grill just over the coals.

Melt the butter in the hot pan, then add the garlic, followed by the mussels. Cook for a minute, then add the beer. Pop the lid on the pan and allow to steam for 5–6 minutes until the mussels are open and cooked through. Discard any mussels that remain closed.

Season lightly to taste, squeeze over the lemon juice and sprinkle the chopped parsley over the top. Serve at once with some bread for mopping up the juices.

DUCK FAT GARLIC SCALLOPS

It's traditional to cook scallops in a garlic, lemon and herb butter, but cooking them in duck fat is a lovely alternative. You can get duck fat hotter than butter without it burning, thus improving the sear and caramelization on the scallops. I love my scallops with the creamy sweet orange roe left attached.

1 tbsp duck fat

12 scallops with roe

freshly squeezed juice of ½ lemon

1 clove garlic, finely chopped

1 tbsp freshly chopped flat-leaf parsley

coarse sea salt and freshly ground black pepper

cast-iron or heavy-duty pan

Serves 2

Set up your barbecue for direct cooking at a moderate heat (around 160–180°C/320–356°F).

Place your pan directly on the coals or close to them on a grill. Allow the pan to warm up a few minutes.

Add the duck fat to the hot pan. After 20–30 seconds, when the fat is sizzling, add the scallops. Cook for 2–3 minutes until seared and caramelized, then turn to sear and caramelize the other side. Add the lemon juice and garlic for the final minute of cooking, then, once cooked, add the parsley and season with a pinch of salt and pepper. Serve at once.

MAPLE AND CHILLI/CHILI SCALLOPS WITH BEETROOT/ BEETS AND KALE

Scallops are plump and sweet, but a glaze of light maple syrup and some fruity chilli flakes/hot red pepper flakes really complement their flavour. The beetroot/ beets have a delicious earthy sweetness and the kale, when crisp, resembles seaweed.

2 small beetroot/beets

8 scallops with roe

4 tsp maple syrup

1 tsp Aleppo chilli flakes/hot red pepper flakes

a handful of kale

1 tsp extra virgin olive oil, plus extra to drizzle

coarse sea salt

lemon wedges, to serve

2 flat metal skewers

Serves 2

Set up your barbecue for direct cooking at a high heat (around 180°C/356°F).

Place the beetroot/beets directly into the embers and cook for around 20–30 minutes until the outside is charred and the inside softened, then set aside until cool enough to handle.

Thread four scallops onto each skewer and season with salt.

Cook the scallops over direct heat for 3–4 minutes on each side until lightly brown.

Lightly brush the scallops with the maple syrup using a pastry or silicon brush and dust with the chilli flakes/hot red pepper flakes, then cook for a minute more on each side, ensuring the internal temperature doesn't go higher than 55°C/131°F.

Toss the kale in the olive oil and place directly over the coals to crisp up (you can use a metal sieve/strainer placed onto the coals for this).

Thinly slice the beetroot/beets.

Plate up the beetroot/beet slices, crispy kale and scallops, season with a pinch of sea salt and drizzle with a little olive oil. Serve with lemon wedges for squeezing over.

BUCKET SEAFOOD BOIL

If you're cooking a seafood feast for a group of friends and family, you don't want to be fiddling around with small, delicate pieces of fish – you want to go big. Cooking up a whole load of super-fresh seafood in a bucket or two, and pouring it out with a flourish onto a large platter for everyone to get stuck into is a real treat for a special occasion.

1.5 kg/3¼ lb. live mussels, debearded

12 langoustines or large prawns/jumbo shrimp

8 crab claws

a selection of any other seafood you'd like, such as clams, squid rings or cockles

2 corn cobs/ears, cut in half

4 cloves garlic, finely chopped

100 g/7 tbsp butter

2 lemons, quartered

500 ml/2 cups medium cider

a handful of freshly chopped flat-leaf parsley

coarse sea salt and freshly ground black pepper

chunks of rustic bread, such as focaccia or sourdough, to serve

large, clean stainless-steel bucket, ideally with a lid

Serves 4

Set up an open barbecue or fire pit with a couple of handfuls of charcoal or cook on the embers of a hardwood/fruitwood fire.

Place all of the seafood and corn cobs/ears in the bucket. Add half of the garlic, half of the butter and one of the lemon quarters, and season with a couple of pinches of salt and pepper. Pour over the cider. Place the lid on or seal the top with foil.

Place the bucket onto the coals and bring to the boil. Cook for around 10–15 minutes, stirring a couple of times during cooking – the prawns/shrimp should be pink, the crab claws should be red and the mussels (and clams and cockles, if using) should be open. Discard any shellfish that haven't opened and ensure all the seafood is cooked through.

Melt the rest of the butter in a pan and stir in the remaining garlic and the parsley.

Pour the contents of the bucket onto a large platter and pour over the garlic butter. Serve with the lemon quarters for squeezing over and some chunks of bread to dip in the juices.

GRILLED GARLIC BUTTER LANGOUSTINES

Langoustines are a real treat. Here they are cooked simply on a hot grill and smothered in a garlic, herb and lemon butter. They are sweet and delicious.

Set up your barbecue for direct cooking at a high heat (around 180–200°C/356–392°F).

Place the langoustines on the grill and cook over direct heat for 5–6 minutes, turning occasionally, until they have an internal temperature of 55–60°C/131–140°F. Season with salt and pepper and set aside.

Melt the butter in the pan and add the garlic, lemon juice and parsley.

Arrange the langoustines on a platter or two plates and pour over the melted garlic, herb and lemon butter.

Serve at once with lemon wedges.

20 langoustines

50 g/3½ tbsp butter

1 clove garlic, finely chopped

freshly squeezed juice of
½ lemon

2 tbsp freshly chopped flat-leaf
parsley

coarse sea salt and freshly
ground black pepper

lemon wedges, to serve

small cast-iron or heavy-duty pan

Serves 2

PRAWNS/SHRIMP WITH 'NDUJA AND LIME

I love large prawns/jumbo shrimp with a charred shell cooked over a high heat, but a little fatty, spicy, melted 'nduja (spicy, spreadable pork sausage) butter and a squeeze of fresh lime juice makes them particularly delicious.

240 g/8½ oz. large shell-on prawns or wild red shrimp

1 tbsp light olive oil

30 g/2 tbsp butter

2 tbsp 'nduja

freshly squeezed juice of 1 lime

1 tbsp freshly chopped flat-leaf parsley

coarse sea salt and freshly ground black pepper

crusty bread, to serve

small cast-iron or heavy-duty pan

Serves 2

Set up your barbecue for direct cooking at a high heat (around 200°C/392°F).

Toss the prawns/shrimp in the oil and season lightly.

Place the prawns/shrimp on the grill for a few minutes, then turn and continue to cook until they are pink, cooked through and the shells charred. Set aside.

Melt the butter and 'nduja together in the cast-iron pan over the barbecue. Add the prawns/shrimp and stir to coat, then squeeze over the lime and sprinkle over the flat-leaf parsley.

Serve with crusty bread to mop up the pan juices.

OCTOPUS WITH 'NDUJA

Octopus isn't something you see all the time, but it lends itself perfectly to grilling over hot coals. It does, however, need a bit of prep to ensure it is tender. The best octopus, if you can get it, is the double-suckered Mediterranean version, which is sometimes available precooked and vacuum-packed. A fresh octopus will require cleaning and boiling in salted water for an hour, then allowed to cool before grilling. The octopus goes lovely and crispy with a bit of the spicy 'nduja butter brushed on — it's so good (see page 67).

Set up your barbecue for direct cooking at a high heat (around 180–200°C/356–392°F).

Lightly oil the octopus tentacles and season well with salt and pepper.

Melt the butter and 'nduja together in the pan and stir to mix. Set aside.

Grill the octopus tentacles over direct heat until crisp on the outside; about 8–10 minutes.

Brush on the 'nduja butter and squeeze over one of the lemon quarters, then continue to cook until the octopus reaches an internal temperature of 60–65°C/140–149°F.

Serve with the remaining lemon quarters to squeeze over the top, and with some grilled greens of your choice alongside.

2 or 4 precooked octopus tentacles

3 tbsp extra virgin olive oil

15 g/1 tbsp butter

1 tbsp 'nduja

1 lemon, quartered

coarse sea salt and freshly ground black pepper

grilled greens, to serve

small cast-iron or heavy-duty pan

Serves 2

HOT-SMOKED MACKEREL PATÉ

A light and flavourful hot smoked mackerel paté is a real treat in summer when mackerel is plentiful. Hot-smoking with a light fruity wood, such as cherry, gives great colour and flavour, but feel free to use your favourite smoking wood. Smoking it yourself will create a much better flavour than any commercial hot-smoked mackerel. Serve with crusty buttered toast or on Little Gem/Bibb lettuce boats.

To hot smoke your mackerel, first you need to lightly cure them. Place the cleaned and gutted mackerel on a non-reactive plate or tray. Mix together the salt and sugar, and sprinkle it evenly over the mackerel. Cover and place in the fridge overnight to cure.

The next morning wipe off any excess salt and sugar.

Set up your barbecue for lid-on indirect cooking at a low heat (around 100–120°C/212–248°F), with a chunk or two of cherry wood on the coals for smoke.

Smoke your mackerel on the barbecue over indirect heat with the lid on for around 1–1½ hours until they reach an internal temperature of 60°C/140°F.

Allow the mackerel to cool for an hour, then flake off the cooked smoky flesh, discarding any bones.

Mix the mackerel with the crème fraîche, horseradish sauce, a squeeze of lemon juice and some salt and pepper. Sprinkle over the flat-leaf parsley and then cover and place in the fridge to chill until you are ready to serve.

2 mackerel, cleaned and gutted

2 tbsp fine salt

2 tbsp demerara sugar

4 tbsp crème fraîche

2 tsp horseradish sauce

a squeeze of lemon juice

3 tbsp freshly chopped flat-leaf parsley

coarse sea salt and freshly ground black pepper

Little Gem/Bibb lettuce leaves or toast, to serve

Serves 4

SPICY FISH BURGER

Here, some simply cooked white fish with a hit of spice is loaded into a brioche bun with a handful of salad leaves – it makes for a tasty yet simple fish burger. Use whichever white fish looks good at the fishmonger. I went for haddock, but cod or pollock will also work well.

200-g/7-oz. skinless and boneless white fish fillet

1 tbsp coarse sea salt

1 tsp olive oil, plus extra for cooking (optional)

a pinch of Aleppo chilli flakes/ hot red pepper flakes

2 brioche buns

a handful of salad leaves

Sriracha mayo, to drizzle

freshly ground black pepper

cast-iron or heavy-duty pan (optional)

Serves 2

Set up your barbecue for direct cooking at a moderate heat (around 160–180°C/320–356°F).

Cut the fish fillet in half to create two thinner fillets. Pop these on a non-reactive plate. Sprinkle the sea salt over both sides of the fish, cover and refrigerate for a couple of hours to cure slightly and firm up.

Rinse off any salt from the fish and pat dry with paper towels. Rub the olive oil into the fish and season with a pinch of black pepper and the chilli flakes/hot red pepper flakes.

Either cook the fish directly on the grill or in a cast-iron pan with a little olive oil for a few minutes on each side until cooked through – it should have an internal temperature of 55–60°C/131–140°F.

Toast the buns, then load each bun up with salad and fish fillet. Drizzle over the Sriracha mayo and serve at once.

SEA BREAM WITH CHIMICHURRI ROJO

We're blessed with some wonderful seafood, but many people struggle with cooking it on a barbecue without it sticking and falling apart. In order to stop these problems, the best trick it to prevent the fish from touching the grill. One of my favourite techniques is to suspend the fish on skewers over the coals.

2 sea bream, cleaned and gutted

1 lemon

coarse sea salt and freshly ground black pepper

CHIMICHURRI ROJO

2 cloves garlic

a handful of freshly chopped flat-leaf parsley and oregano

1 tbsp dried oregano

60 ml/4 tbsp extra virgin olive oil, plus extra if needed

a pinch of smoked paprika

2 tbsp red wine vinegar

1 tbsp tomato purée/paste

2 long, flat metal skewers

Serves 2

Set up your barbecue for direct cooking, so that you can suspend a couple of long skewers about 15–20 cm/6–8 in. above the embers without touching the grate. A couple of bricks with the coals between them would work at a push. The heat at the cooking level should be hot enough that you can only hold your hand (carefully) at this level for 2–3 seconds.

Skewer a gutted sea bream onto each skewer, from the mouth down to the tail. Halve the lemon, then cut a slice from each half. Place a slice of lemon inside the cavity of each fish, then thread what's left of the lemon halves onto the ends of the skewers. Season the skin of the fish with plenty of coarse sea salt and black pepper.

Suspend the fish over the coals and cook for 6–7 minutes until the skin crisps and chars slightly, then turn the skewer over and cook the other side for 6–7 minutes until the fish is cooked through – it should have an internal temperature of 55–60°C/131–140°F.

Make a quick chimichurri rojo by blitzing up all the ingredients with a good pinch of coarse sea salt in a mini chopper, food processor or blender until you have a fairly smooth paste. Loosen up with a little more olive oil, if you wish.

Serve the sea bream with the chimichurro rojo.

SKATE WINGS WITH CHERMOULA

Skate wings are really delicious with a crisp char on the outside from being cooked on the barbecue. Most skate wings are actually ray wings, sold as skate wings. Chermoula is a North African condiment, similar in a way to salsa verde or chimichurri, but it is made with coriander/cilantro and a hint of cumin. It works perfectly with fish.

2 skate wings

2 tbsp olive oil

coarse sea salt and freshly ground black pepper

CHERMOULA

50 g/1¾ oz. coriander/cilantro

20 g/¾ oz. flat-leaf parsley

2 cloves garlic

1 tsp grated lemon zest

80 ml/⅓ cup olive oil

½ tsp flaky sea salt

¼ tsp paprika

¼ tsp cumin powder

½ tsp Aleppo chilli flakes/hot red pepper flakes

freshly squeezed juice of ½ lemon

Serves 2

Set up your barbecue for lid-on direct cooking at a moderate heat (around 160–180°C/320–356°F).

Dry off the outside of the skate wing with paper towels, then lightly rub with the olive oil and season with salt and pepper.

Blitz up all the ingredients for the chermoula in a mini chopper, food processor or blender (or chop them first and then use a mortar and pestle to blend) until they form a thick paste.

Place the seasoned skate wings on the grill above the coals and cook with the lid on for 4–5 minutes, then turn over and cook on the other side until both sides are lightly charred and the fish is cooked through – the wings should have an internal temperature of 60°C/140°F.

Serve at once, drizzled with the zingy chermoula.

LOG-SMOKED SALMON

A fabulous technique for ensuring that you don't have any issues with fish sticking to the grill and falling apart is the plank cooking technique. But you don't have to use a thin plank of wood to cook on; some of my best fish is cooked on top of a split log, such as silver birch, ash or cherry, and then surrounded by coals. The coals get the log smouldering on the edges to infuse the fish with delicious smoke and to cook the fish through. Enjoy with a fresh green salad and some new potatoes.

3 lemons

a handful of fresh herbs, such as oregano, thyme or marjoram

1 side of salmon, around 800 g–1 kg/1¾–2¼ lb.

3 tbsp runny honey

coarse sea salt and freshly ground black pepper

large split hardwood or fruitwood log (big enough for the salmon fillet to sit on)

Serves 4

Set up your barbecue for lid-on cooking at a moderate heat (around 150–160°C/302–320°F). Light the charcoal, then add another couple of handfuls and spread it out.

Thinly slice two of the lemons. Place the herbs (reserving just a few for sprinkling on top) and half of the lemon slices on the split log, then place the side of salmon on top. Season the fish lightly with salt and black pepper, and place the remaining lemon slices along the middle of the fillet. Sprinkle over the reserved herbs.

Pop the log with the salmon on top of the coals, close the barbecue lid and cook for around 15–20 minutes.

Make up a honey and lemon glaze by mixing the honey with the juice of the third lemon in a small bowl.

Once the internal temperature of the salmon fillet has reached 50°C/122°F, brush the top of the fillet with the honey and lemon glaze using a pastry or silicon brush.

Cook for another 8–10 minutes, glazing another two or three times, if you like. The salmon is cooked when the internal temperature of the thickest part reaches 55°C/131°F.

Using thick heatproof gloves, remove the log with the cooked salmon fillet from the barbecue and place it on the serving table on top of a heatproof surface. Serve.

ALDER-SMOKED COD

Alder creates a really interesting smoke. It's got a nice balance of sweet and savoury elements and gives food a lovely yellowish-brown colour. It works perfectly with white fish, such as cod.

Set up your barbecue for lid-on cooking at a low–moderate heat (around 120–140°C/248–284°F). Add a handful of alder wood chips or a chunk of alder wood on the charcoal to smoke.

Place the lemon slices and herbs on the soaked cedar plank and then top with the cod fillets. Season the fish with salt and pepper. If you don't have a plank, place the ingredients onto a piece of foil, but don't wrap the fish in the foil as you want the smoke to reach the fish.

Place in the barbecue, close the lid and smoke for around 40 minutes until the fish reaches an internal temperature of 55–60°C/131–140°F.

Using thick heatproof gloves, remove the plank with the cooked fish from the barbecue and place it on the serving table on top of a heatproof surface. Serve.

1 lemon, thinly sliced

a handful of fresh herbs, such as oregano or thyme

2 cod fillet portions

coarse sea salt and freshly ground black pepper

cedar plank (big enough for the cod fillets to sit on), soaked (optional)

Serves 2

PLANKED DOVER SOLE

The fish most commonly cooked on a plank of wood is a salmon fillet, but it works really well for flat fish, such as plaice and sole. Here I went for a delicious Dover sole with fresh herbs and lemon slices. I nailed the sole to an oak plank using thick wrought-iron nails, which can easily be purchased online, and cooked it at an angle over the embers on a firepit. To support the plank at an angle near the heat, you can hammer in a wooden pole next to your firepit and lash the top of the plank to it. You can also cook this on your barbecue.

1 lemon, thinly sliced

a handful of fresh herbs, such as sprigs of oregano and thyme

1 Dover sole

1 tbsp olive oil

coarse sea salt and freshly ground black pepper

oak or cedar plank, soaked (optional)

thick wrought-iron nails (optional)

Serves 2

Set up an open fire at a moderate heat (around 160°C/320°F) so that you can set up the plank of wood at an angle to the edge of the heat. Alternatively, set up your barbecue for lid-on direct cooking at a moderate heat (around 160–180°C/320–356°F).

Arrange some of the lemon slices and herbs along the plank, if using, then place the sole on top, dark-side up. Use the nails to secure the fish to the plank. Rub the olive oil into the fish skin and season.

Cook for around 15–20 minutes until the skin crisps up and the fish is cooked through – it should have an internal temperature of 55–60°C/131–140°F.

You can either remove the fish from the plank, or, as is my preference, serve the fish on the plank at the table.

SEABASS WRAPPED IN LEEK

A large leek can be opened out by cutting it lengthways on one side only, which creates a fantastic wrapper for delicate fish and stops it from sticking to the grill. Here I went for some fresh seabass, which can be quite delicate and fall apart if it sticks to the grill. Using a leek 'wrapper' adds an extra delicious dimension as the leek chars up.

1 large leek

1 lemon, thinly sliced

1 seabass (about 700 g/ 1½ lb.), cleaned and gutted, or 2 seabass fillets

coarse sea salt and freshly ground black pepper

wooden skewer, soaked in water

Serves 2

Set up your barbecue for lid-on indirect cooking at a high heat (around 180–200°C/356–392°F).

Take the leek and run a sharp knife from top to bottom, only cutting to the middle, not all the way through. Open out the leek sheets.

Stuff a couple of slices of lemon into the cavity of the fish or place them between the fillets. Season the skin.

Wrap a few of the leek sheets around the fish, tucking them in and using the soaked wooden skewer to secure.

Place the fish on the grill (the leek sheets will stop the fish sticking to the grill, making it easy to turn). Cook over indirect heat for 20–30 minutes, turning occasionally, until cooked through – it should have an internal temperature of 55–60°C/131–140°F.

Serve at once.

MAPLE-GLAZED SMOKED TROUT

I remember a great trip to Vancouver many years ago, where I enjoyed a treat called Indian candy — basically smoked-cured salmon chunks with a thick glaze of maple syrup on the outside. Absolutely something you can't stop eating. I had some plump trout fillets and decided to recreate the Indian candy, but with trout. And it was equally delicious.

The night before you plan to smoke the fish, it needs to be lightly cured. Place the trout in a non-reactive bowl. Mix together the salt and sugar, and sprinkle it evenly over the trout. Cover and place in the fridge overnight to cure.

The next morning wipe off any excess salt and sugar.

Set up your barbecue for lid-on indirect cooking at a low heat (around 80–100°C/176–212°F), with a chunk or two of cherry wood on the coals for smoke.

Smoke the trout on the barbecue over indirect heat with the lid on for around 30 minutes until the fish reaches an internal temperature of 40°C/104°F.

Brush over the maple syrup with a pastry or silicon brush and continue to cook for another 30 minutes or so, lightly building up the glaze every few minutes, until the internal temperature of the fish hits 55–60°C/131–140°F.

Remove from the barbecue and rest for as long as you can resist. Serve hot or cold.

2 trout or salmon fillets

50 g/scant ¼ cup fine sea salt

50 g/¼ cup Demerara/raw sugar

90 ml/6 tbsp good-quality maple syrup

Serves 2

SUSPENDED WHOLE PLAICE

A delicate fish such as a plaice can easily stick to the grill and fall to pieces while you're cooking. Suspending the fish on skewers over the hot coals is a great way to avoid this, as it doesn't ever touch the grill, but you still get lovely, crispy, charred skin, and it's easy to turn. A lovely fresh fish is best cooked and served simply, and this is a great technique for a fuss-free meal.

Set up your barbecue for direct cooking at a moderate heat (around 160–180°C/320–356°F).

Stuff the fish cavity with a couple of slices of lemon. Push the two skewers through the fish lengthways, then rub the fish with the olive oil and season it with salt and pepper.

Cook over direct heat for 10–12 minutes, turning as required, until the skin is crispy and charred and the fish is cooked through – it should have an internal temperature of 55–60°C/131–140°F.

Serve at once.

1 plaice

1 lemon, thinly sliced

1 tbsp olive oil

coarse sea salt and freshly ground black pepper

2 long, flat metal skewers

Serves 2

BUTTER-SPICED MONKFISH FILLET

Monkfish is a great fish to cook on the barbecue using direct grilling. It's firm enough not to fall apart like a lot of the more delicate fish, and, with a spiced crust and a bit of sear, it tastes really special.

1 monkfish tail, about 400–500 g/14 oz.–1 lb. 2 oz., skin and bone removed

30 g/2 tbsp softened butter

1 tsp garam masala or similar spice mix

1 tsp cumin seeds

1 tsp turmeric powder

1 lemon, quartered

1 tbsp freshly chopped coriander/cilantro

a pinch of chilli flakes/hot red pepper flakes

sea salt and freshly ground black pepper

Serves 2

Set up your barbecue for lid-on two-zone (direct and indirect) cooking at a moderate heat (around 160–180°C/320–356°F).

Lightly season the outside of the monkfish tail with salt and pepper.

Put the softened butter in a bowl, add the spices and squeeze in one of the lemon quarters. Mix to make a spiced butter.

Sear the outside of the monkfish fillet over the coals, then brush on the spiced butter with a pastry or silicon brush. Cook with the barbecue lid on, turning the fish as required during cooking and brushing with a little more butter each time you do so. Once the monkfish is charred, you can move it to a cooler part of the grill and cook over indirect heat until the internal temperature of the monkfish reaches 55–60°C/131–140°F.

Allow to rest a few minutes, then slice the fish thickly, squeeze over the rest of the lemon quarters and sprinkle with the chopped coriander/cilantro and chilli flakes/hot red pepper flakes.

GRILLED MACKEREL WITH ZHOUG

I fell in love with tangy zhoug sauce from Yemen after tasting it for the first time. It's kind of a Middle Eastern, coriander/cilantro-rich condiment that has a bit of a kick. It went so well combined with these charred fresh mackerel.

4 very fresh whole mackerel, cleaned and gutted

1 lemon, quartered

coarse sea salt and freshly ground black pepper

ZHOUG

a handful of coriander/cilantro, around 30 g/1 oz.

a small handful of flat-leaf parsley, around 20 g/¾ oz.

1 green chilli/chile

1 plump clove garlic

1 tsp cumin powder

a small pinch of cumin seeds

freshly squeezed juice of ½ lemon

1 tsp Aleppo chilli flakes/hot red pepper flakes

80 ml/⅓ cup extra virgin olive oil

4 long, flat metal skewers

Serves 4

Make up the zhoug by blitzing up all the ingredients into a fine sauce using a stick blender or crush them together using a mortar and pestle.

Set up your barbecue for direct cooking at a high heat (around 180–200°C/356–392°F).

Season the mackerel generously with salt and pepper.

Skewer the whole fish on the flat metal skewers (long enough to rest on the edges of the barbecue so the fish is suspended over the grill to prevent it sticking).

Cook the mackerel directly over the heat, turning the skewers every few minutes and squeezing a little of the lemon over the fish, until the skin is crisp and charred and the fish is cooked through with an internal temperature of 55–60°C/131–140°F.

Serve at once with a drizzle of the zingy zhoug and the remaining lemon quarters for squeezing over.

CHAPTER 3

MOSTLY MEAT

ARROZ CON POLLO

A simple version of a paella, this Spanish-style rice with chicken has to be one of my family's most asked-for meals. It's a great way to cook for a crowd, and looks wonderful when placed in the middle of the table.

12 chicken thighs

3 tbsp extra virgin olive oil

1 onion, finely chopped

2 cloves garlic, finely chopped

1 stick celery, finely chopped

1 red (bell) pepper, finely chopped

1 carrot, finely chopped

150 g/5¼ oz. chorizo, cubed or sliced

420 g/2¼ cups paella rice

1.5 litres/6¼ cups chicken stock

½ tsp smoked paprika

a few strands of saffron

1 lemon, quartered

coarse sea salt and freshly ground black pepper

a handful of freshly chopped flat-leaf parsley, to garnish

paella pan (or large flat pan that will fit in your barbecue with the lid down)

Serves 6

Set up your barbecue for lid-on direct cooking at a moderate heat (around 180°C/356°F).

Season the chicken thighs with salt and pepper, then cook on the barbecue for around 25–30 minutes, skin-side down, until crispy and the internal temperature of the chicken reaches 74°C/165°F. Set aside.

Drizzle the olive oil into the paella pan and add the onion, garlic, celery, red (bell) pepper and carrot. Place the pan on the barbecue and cook until the vegetables are soft. Add the chorizo and continue to cook until it release its oils.

Add the rice and allow to cook for a few minutes, before adding enough of the chicken stock to cover. Add the smoked paprika and saffron and season with salt and pepper. Allow to simmer with the barbecue lid down until most of the liquid has been absorbed, around 20 minutes.

Put the cooked chicken thighs on top of the rice and add the quartered lemon. Turn the heat down and cook for another few minutes until the rice starts to form a slight crust on the bottom of the pan (which is my favourite bit). At this stage, the rice will be cooked perfectly.

Garnish with some chopped flat-leaf parsley and serve.

DIRTY BLACK PUDDING CRUMBLE TOAST

As a child I loved experimenting with my food, and this is certainly still true today! Give me a few ingredients and a fire, and I'll come up with something playful and delicious. This recipe came about with me topping 'dirty toast' (bread toasted in the coals) with a crispy black pudding crumble.

4 slices black pudding

2 tbsp bone marrow

4 slices focaccia, ciabatta or sourdough bread

Sriracha mayo, to drizzle

2 tbsp freshly chopped flat-leaf parsley

coarse sea salt and freshly ground black pepper

cast-iron or heavy-duty pan

Serves 2

Set up your barbecue for direct cooking at moderate heat (around 160–180°C/320–356°F) over quality lumpwood coals or fruitwood/hardwood embers. You should be able to hold your hand (carefully) just over the coals for 3–4 seconds.

Place the cast-iron pan over the coals and crumble in the black pudding. Cook for 8–10 minutes, stirring occasionally, until crispy. Set aside.

Spread ½ tbsp bone marrow lightly onto each piece of bread. Place them, bone-marrow-side down, directly onto the coals to toast – be careful as the bone marrow can flare up and burn the bread, but a little char is a good thing.

Turn the pieces of bread over and toast the other side on the coals. Season the toast with a pinch of sea salt and black pepper.

Plate up the dirty toasts and top each portion with black pudding crumble. Drizzle over the Sriracha mayo and sprinkle over the flat-leaf parsley, then serve.

SMOKED AND BRAISED OXTAIL

Oxtail is a rare sight on a barbecue, usually ending up in a slow cooker or pressure cooker. However, with a bit of smoke and braising in a cast-iron Dutch oven, you really can develop some deeply satisfying and warming flavours.

1 oxtail, cut between the bone into short lengths

2 cloves garlic, finely chopped

1 red onion, thinly sliced

15 g/1 tbsp butter

a handful of fresh woody herbs, such as rosemary, thyme and bay

1 litre/4 cups rich beef stock

coarse sea salt and freshly ground black pepper

2 tbsp Chimichurri Rojo Butter (see page 156)

cast-iron Dutch oven or heavy-duty pan with a lid

Serves 2

Set up your barbecue for lid-on indirect cooking at a low–moderate heat (around 140–150°C/284–302°F) with a chunk of cherry wood for smoke.

Season the oxtail pieces with salt and pepper.

Place the oxtail pieces on the barbecue and smoke over indirect heat for 2 hours with the lid on.

Put the garlic, onion and butter in the Dutch oven and place in the middle of the barbecue. Cook for 8–10 minutes until the onion has caramelized and softened. Add the herbs, oxtail pieces and stock, pop the lid of the Dutch oven on, and then close the lid of the barbecue. Allow to cook for 3 hours until the meat on the oxtail is soft and falling off the bone.

Top with the chimichurri rojo butter and serve from the Dutch oven.

'NDUJA-TOPPED HASSELBACK POTATOES

You could say that I'm a little bit obsessed with 'nduja! This spicy, spreadable, pork-fat salami is a true revelation when you first try it – and very addictive. Fortunately my mate Marc Dennis at Duchy Charcuterie in Cornwall makes the best I've ever tasted. The way it melts when slightly warmed and releases its spicy fat over these hasselback potatoes, running down into the space between the slices, is just sublime.

8 potatoes, all of a similar size

2 tbsp olive oil

4 tbsp 'nduja

2 spring onions/scallions, chopped

coarse sea salt and freshly ground black pepper

Serves 4

Set up your barbecue for lid-on indirect cooking at a high heat (around 180–200°C/356–392°F).

Place two wooden spoons on a chopping board and place a potato in-between the handles. Using a sharp knife, cut down into the potato, using the spoon handles to stop you cutting all the way through. Continue slicing every 3 mm/⅛ in. to create the hasselback effect. Repeat for all of the potatoes.

Drizzle the potatoes with the olive oil and rub it in. Season generously with sea salt and black pepper.

Place the potatoes on the barbecue and cook them over indirect heat with the barbecue lid on for around 40 minutes until the outside is crispy and the potatoes are cooked through.

Serve the potatoes topped with the 'nduja and chopped spring onions/scallions.

SPICED LAMB, FETA AND AUBERGINE/EGGPLANT TARTLETS

These are the meaty equivalent of aubergine/eggplant bruschetta. They follow a similar principle of loading a grilled slice of aubergine/eggplant with delicious toppings – in this case, spiced minced/ground lamb and feta cheese. You can add other toppings, such as sliced olives or some chilli/chile pieces, if you like.

300 g/10½ oz. minced/ground lamb

2 tsp ras el hanout, shawarma or baharat spice

2 large aubergines/eggplants, cut into 2.5-cm/1-in. thick rounds

2–3 tbsp olive oil

200-g/7-oz. block feta cheese

coarse sea salt and freshly ground black pepper

cast-iron or heavy-duty pan

baking sheet that will fit in your barbecue, lined with foil

Serves 4

Set up your barbecue for lid-on, two-zone (direct and indirect) cooking at a moderate heat (around 150–160°C/302–320°F).

Place the cast-iron pan over the direct zone above the coals and add the minced/ground lamb, the spice mix and a pinch of salt and pepper. Cook for 6–8 minutes until browned slightly and cooked through, stirring occasionally so the lamb doesn't burn and cooks evenly. Set aside.

Rub the aubergine/eggplant slices with the olive oil on both sides, and season lightly with salt and pepper. Place the rounds on the foil-lined baking sheet and place on the barbecue. Cook for 8–10 minutes until softened slightly but not mushy.

Top each aubergine/eggplant slice with some cooked spiced lamb and crumble a little feta on top. Cook with the barbecue lid on for a further 6–8 minutes, the serve.

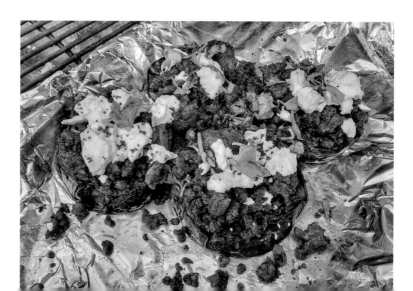

STINKING BISHOP-STUFFED BURGER

I first cooked a Stinking Bishop-stuffed burger many years ago, but I wanted to recreate this wonderful dish for this book. Stinking Bishop, as its name suggests, is a strong pungent cheese, but it is also very creamy and works really nicely with dry-aged beef. The cheese goes really melty and oozy.

Set up your barbecue for cooking on a hot plate or in a cast-iron pan at a high heat (around 180–200°C/356–392°F).

Take two of the patties and place half of the cheese in-between them. Press the patties together to seal the cheese in the middle. Repeat with the remaining patties and cheese.

Sear the burgers on the hot plate or cast-iron pan, and cook on both sides until the meat is cooked through (when it reaches an internal temperature of 74°C/165°F) and the cheese has melted. Remove and set aside.

Add the onion and butter to the hot plate or pan and cook until charred and soft.

Serve the burgers on toasted brioche buns with the charred onions and some piccalilli for a powerfully-flavoured juicy burger.

4 thin dry-aged beef patties or 400 g/14 oz. minced/ground dry-aged beef shaped into 4 patties

60 g/2 oz. Stinking Bishop or other strong cheese, grated

1 onion, thinly sliced

15 g/1 tbsp butter

2 brioche burger buns

2 tbsp piccalilli

hot plate or cast-iron pan

Serves 2

PIZZA'D CHICKEN DRUMSTICKS

What do you get when you cross a chicken drumstick with a pizza? I'm not great at jokes, but thankfully I'm better at coming up with recipes! Butterflied chicken drumsticks have become a feature on social media over the last couple of years. The flattened-out shape of a butterflied chicken drumstick is the perfect mini 'pizza' base with a built-in handle.

Set up your barbecue for lid-on direct cooking at a moderate heat (around 160–180°C/320–356°F). I added a small handful of cherry wood chips to the coals, to give a subtle sweet smoke.

Butterfly the chicken drumsticks by running a small sharp knife down one side of the drumstick, right down to the bone, then butterflying out the meat without detaching it from the bone.

Season both sides of the chicken drumsticks with a pinch of salt and pepper and the mixed herbs. Placed the seasoned chicken drumsticks on the grill skin-side down and cook with the lid on for around 20 minutes until the skin is crispy.

Turn the drumsticks over and cook for a further 10 minutes until the chicken has reached an internal temperature of 74°C/165°F.

Turn the drumsticks back over (so they are skin-side down) and top the meat side of each drumstick with 1 tsp tomato purée/paste and spread this around with the spoon. Top each drumstick generously with mozzarella and a slice of pepperoni.

Close the lid and cook for another 5–10 minutes until the cheese melts. Serve at once.

4 chicken drumsticks

1 tsp dried mixed herbs

4 tsp tomato purée/paste

60 g/⅔ cup grated mozzarella cheese

4 slices pepperoni

coarse sea salt and freshly ground black pepper

Serves 2

COFFEE, RUM AND MAPLE-GLAZED PORK CHOPS

A good pork chop is a wonderful thing, but not easy to get right. You need the right sort of heat to ensure a good sear and crispy crackling. I love to cook pork chops over wood embers — have a searing hot side with a few flames (to which I add new wood) and a bed of embers on the other side. Here I used an Argentine-style firepit grill but you can use your regular barbecue.

2 pork chops, about 4–5 cm/
1½–2 in. thick

25 ml/1¾ tbsp/1 shot freshly
brewed espresso coffee

25 ml/1¾ tbsp/1 shot rum

2 tbsp maple syrup

coarse sea salt and freshly
ground black pepper

Serves 2

For this recipe, you're looking to use a good, high-heat-output wood, such as ash, silver birch or beech. Build your fire using a Jenga method of stacking 7.5–10-cm/3–4-in. diameter splits. Light it using a natural firelighter — I place one in the top and one in the bottom of the stack. Allow to burn down, adding new wood of the same size as needed.

Set up your firepit or barbecue for direct cooking about 15–20 cm/6–8 in. above the embers. The heat at grill level should be hot enough that you can only hold your hand (carefully) at the grill level for 2–3 seconds.

Cut the rind of the pork chops at intervals of every 5 cm/2 in. to stop the chops curling up as the crackling forms. Season with plenty of salt and black pepper.

Place the first chop on the grill and hold it, with some tongs, skin-edge down, over the hottest part of the grill until the crackling bubbles up. Repeat for the second chop, then lay both chops flat on the grill and sear both sides, moving them from the hotter to the cooler part of the grill so as not to burn them.

Make up a glaze by mixing together the espresso, rum and maple syrup.

Glaze the seared chops using a pastry or silicon brush, then continue to glaze them every few minutes. Cook the chops for about 15 minutes until they are cooked through but still juicy (and have reached an internal temperature of 63°C/145°F).

Allow to rest for a few minutes and enjoy.

BUTTER-SPICED TURKEY

So many people dismiss turkey as a bland, dry and unexciting meat, but if cooked to the correct internal temperature it stays juicy. Baste it with a spicy butter and it's far from bland. I was hugely inspired by my good friend Nila Ross-Patel who runs Indian barbecue classes at UK BBQ School – she cooked the most amazing butter-stuffed turkey breast as part of her practice run for a Christmas class. This is a simplified, yet still delicious version of her recipe.

Set up your barbecue for lid-on indirect cooking at a high heat (around 180°C/356°F).

Place the turkey breast, skin-side up, on a baking sheet that will fit in your barbecue with the lid on.

Melt the butter and stir in the spice mix and turmeric. Brush the spiced butter onto the turkey breast using a pastry or silicon brush and season with salt and pepper.

Place the baking sheet with the turkey in the barbecue and cook over indirect heat for around 40 minutes with the lid on, brushing occasionally with the spiced butter. The internal temperature should reach 74°C/165°F. Remove from the barbecue and let it rest for a good 20 minutes.

Slice the turkey breast and serve garnished with coriander/cilantro.

1 turkey breast, about 1.5–2 kg/3¼–4½ lb.

100 g/7 tbsp salted butter

2 tsp masala spice mix (I used a korma spice mix as my kids like it mild)

2 tsp turmeric powder

coarse sea salt and freshly ground black pepper

a handful of coriander/cilantro, to garnish

Serves 4-6

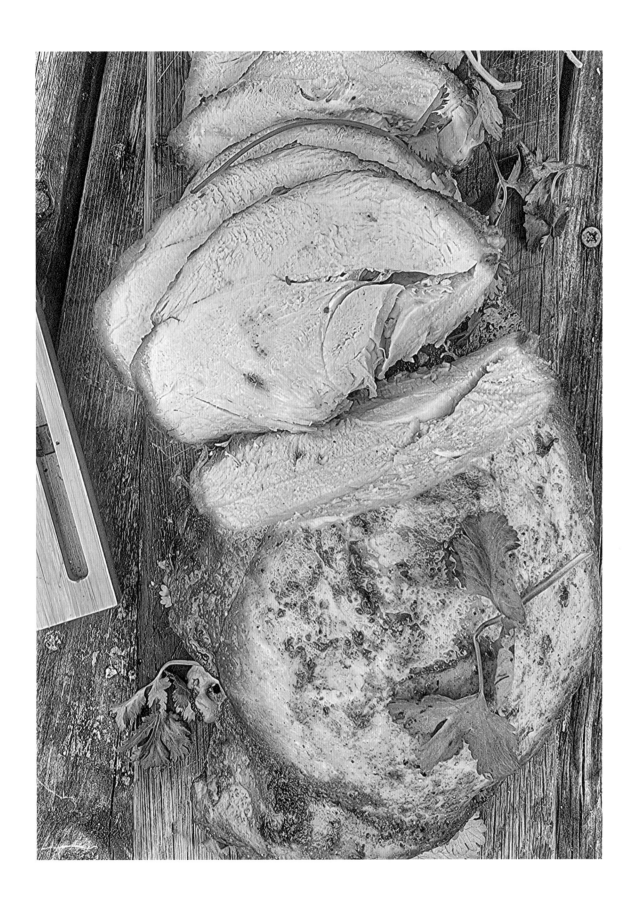

SMOKY SWEET DUCK LEGS

All too often with duck, it's the breast that gets most attention when it comes to cooking, but the leg meat is dark, juicy and delicious. It needs a lot more cooking than the breast, otherwise it remains tough, but if you get the temperature just right it will be amazing. It works perfectly with a touch of cherry or beech smoke, and a sweet glaze. Lot of people think of hot smoking as a lower temperature technique, but adding smoke to roasting meat makes it even more tasty with the additional benefit of crispy skin.

2 duck legs

2 tbsp runny honey

1 tsp Aleppo chilli flakes/hot red pepper flakes

coarse sea salt and freshly ground black pepper

salad leaves, to serve

Serves 2

Set up your barbecue for lid-on direct cooking at a moderate heat (around 160–180°C/320–356°F). Add a chunk of beech or cherry wood for smoke.

Using a sharp knife, pierce the skin all over the duck legs to help the fat render and the skin to crisp up. Season the duck legs with coarse sea salt and black pepper.

Cook the duck legs just to the edge of the direct heat, skin-side down, over a tray to catch the duck fat (perfect for cooking roast potatoes or the Duck Fat Garlic Scallops on page 59). Cook with the lid on for around 40 minutes until the duck reaches an internal temperature of around 85°C/185°F, at which point some of the collagen will have broken down to make the meat tender.

Mix together the honey and chilli flakes/hot red pepper flakes and brush this mixture onto the smoked duck legs. Smoke the legs with the lid down for 5–10 minutes for the glaze to set, then serve with salad leaves.

HANGER STEAKS WITH DIRTY BASTE AND KING OYSTER MUSHROOMS

I'm such a lover of hanger steaks. They might not be the prettiest cut, but they are full of flavour. They can sometimes be hard to get hold of, but are worth seeking out. Here, I pair them up with some delicious king oyster mushrooms cooked in butter and a lovely 'dirty' baste, made with fresh herbs, garlic and anchovy.

4 king oyster mushrooms

a knob/pat of butter

2 hanger steaks, about 400 g/ 14 oz. each, trimmed

Aleppo chilli flakes/hot red pepper flakes, to taste

coarse sea salt

DIRTY BASTE

2 cloves garlic

a handful of rosemary

a handful of thyme

a handful of flat-leaf parsley

150 ml/⅔ cup olive oil

1 anchovy fillet

freshly squeezed juice of ½ lemon

1 tbsp coarse sea salt

cast-iron or heavy-duty pan

Serves 2

For the dirty baste, blitz up the garlic, herbs, olive oil, anchovy and lemon juice in a blender until it forms a baste.

Set up your barbecue for direct cooking at a high heat (around 180–200°C/356–392°F).

Slice the king oyster mushrooms into strips and place in the cast-iron pan with the butter. Cook over the heat until browned, then set aside.

Grill the hanger steaks over direct heat, basting the charred surface with the baste every time you turn the steaks. Cook until the internal temperature is 47°C/117°F for rare, 52°C/126°F for medium-rare or 60°C/140°F for medium (these steaks toughen up above this temperature, so don't go past medium).

Remove from the heat and let them rest for a few minutes.

Serve the steaks with slices of mushroom and a drizzle of the remaining baste over the top. Sprinkle over some sea salt and chilli flakes/hot red pepper flakes to taste.

PICANHA TACOS

Picanha is a difficult cut of meat to track down. It's a prime cut of beef from the top of the rump. A lot of butchers prefer to keep the rump cap as part of the rump, as removing it devalues the overall quality of the rump, as it's the best bit. But if you can befriend your local butcher and persuade them to remove one whole for you, then you are in for a real treat. The picanha is the favourite cut of many steak-lovers in Brazil, and with good reason; it's very juicy, tender and has a lovely taste and texture.

1–1.5-kg/2¼–3¼-lb. picanha/rump cap (see recipe introduction)

16 flour or corn tortillas

a few handfuls of watercress

coarse sea salt

hot sauce of your choice, to serve

cast-iron or heavy-duty pan

Serves 4

I cooked these on a parilla grill (Argentinian-style grill) over birch wood embers. Burn some logs in the brasero fire basket and rake the embers across; the more embers, the hotter the grill. You can raise or lower the grill to moderate the heat level. If using a barbecue, set it up for lid-on, two-zone (direct and indirect) cooking at a moderate heat (around 160–180°C/320–356°F).

Sprinkle sea salt over the picanha, then place it whole on the grill and cook it slowly just to the edge of the direct zone until you have built up a nice crust and the internal temperature is 47°C/117°F.

Remove the picanha from the grill and cut it into thick steaks. Drop the grate down closer to the coals and put the steaks back on the grill to sear them on each side over direct heat.

I made some blue corn tortillas on my new chapa press, which worked really well, but you can toast up some ready-made corn or flour tortillas in a hot cast-iron pan over the heat.

Load up the tortillas with some spicy watercress and slices of picanha and add a dash of your preferred hot sauce to serve.

CAMEMBERT WITH 'NDUJA

Baked Camembert cheese is wonderfully simple to cook on the barbecue, but you can turn it into something even more luxurious by adding a topping of 'nduja, the spicy spreadable salami originating from Calabria in Italy. It really lifts the richness of the Camembert as it melts.

Set up your barbecue for lid-on indirect cooking at a moderate heat (around 160°C/320°F). Add a chunk of cherry wood to the coals for a little smoke

Remove the wrapper from the Camembert, and return it to the wooden box. Spread the 'nduja over the surface. Poke the rosemary sprigs into the cheese as shown and place the whole thing on the barbecue.

Cook over indirect heat with the lid on for about 15–20 minutes, until the Camembert starts to puff up, and you'll probably see some of the cheese start to ooze out.

Serve at once with toasted rustic bread for dipping.

1 Camembert cheese

2 tbsp 'nduja

3 sprigs of rosemary

toasted rustic bread, to serve

Serves 2

SAUSAGE CASSEROLE

Although I first cooked this recipe in a wood-fired oven, you can definitely cook it on a barbecue with a lid. This is a hearty autumnal/fall meal, but it can be lovely and warming on a chilly evening all year round. You'll need a heavy-duty cast-iron pan to cook this in.

3 tbsp olive oil

12 sausages of your choice
(I went for some nice herby
sausages)

1 onion, sliced

1 clove garlic, finely chopped

15 g/1 tbsp butter

1 tbsp plain/all-purpose flour

1 vegetable stock pot

2 tbsp tomato purée/paste

400-g/14-oz. can butter beans,
drained

1 tsp mixed herbs

1 jar passata/strained tomatoes

1 large sweet potato, thinly
sliced

coarse sea salt and freshly
ground black pepper

rustic bread, to serve

cast-iron or heavy-duty pan

Serves 4

Set up your barbecue for lid-on cooking at a high heat (around 180–200°C/356–392°F). You can also use a wood-fired oven.

Add 2 tbsp olive oil and the sausages to the cast-iron pan and place over the heat. Close the barbecue lid and cook until the sausages are browned, around 10–12 minutes.

Add the onion and garlic and cook for another 10 minutes until the onion is softened and caramelized.

Add the butter, flour, stock pot and tomato purée/paste and give it a good stir, then add the butter beans, herbs and passata and season with the sea salt and black pepper. Arrange the sweet potato slices on top of the sausages and drizzle over the remaining 1 tbsp olive oil.

Place back on the barbecue, close the lid and cook for around 20 minutes until the sausages are cooked through (have reached an internal temperature of 74°C/165°F) and the sweet potato has softened and caramelized lightly.

Enjoy in a big bowl with some rustic bread to mop up the sauce.

DIRTY STEAK AND SWISS CHARD SANDWICH

A caveman or dirty steak – meaning it is cooked directly on the coals – is just about my favourite way to cook a steak. I went with a lovely dry-aged sirloin with creamy fat for this dish.

500 g/1 lb. 2 oz. sirloin steak

a handful of Swiss chard

1 large sub roll or 4 slices sourdough bread

coarse sea salt and freshly ground black pepper

DIRTY BASTE

2 cloves garlic

3 sprigs rosemary

3 sprigs thyme

a handful of flat-leaf parsley

60 ml/¼ cup olive oil

1 anchovy fillet

a squeeze of lemon juice

3 tbsp coarse sea salt

cast-iron or heavy-duty pan

Serves 2

Set up your barbecue for direct cooking on the coals with best-quality lumpwood charcoal.

For the dirty baste, blitz up the garlic, herbs, olive oil, anchovy, lemon juice and salt in a blender.

Get the coals red hot. Give them a quick blow to remove any surface ash, then place the steak directly onto the coals. Don't fiddle with it. Let it cook for 3–4 minutes, then flip it over and baste with the dirty baste. Cook for a few more minutes until the internal temperature of the steak hits 47°C/117°F (this will give you a rare steak when rested).

Allow the steak to rest for 5 minutes. Meanwhile, sauté the Swiss chard with a little of the dirty baste in the cast-iron pan.

Slice the rested steak and place on the bread. Pile the Swiss chard on top and serve.

BONE MARROW FONDUE

Some recipes linger in your mind for a long time and once you cook them, you can't stop thinking about them. This recipe certainly falls in this category. I've cooked this a few times over the years for special friends, and they always keep talking about it. As a kid I remember loving fondue – pieces of steak dipped into hot oil with a sizzle, cooked briefly, and enjoyed. A barbecue version using melted garlic-and-herb-infused bone marrow was bound to be a winner. You'll need to sweet talk your butcher for the marrow bones.

Set up your barbecue with a handful of lit charcoal in the base.

Scoop out the bone marrow from the bones (a long flat skewer can work well) and place into the cast-iron pan. Do not fill the pan over half-full, as if it is too full the fat may spill onto the coals. Add the garlic clove and herbs to the bone marrow and place the pan directly on the coals to melt the bone marrow. Please be careful when cooking with hot fat near the coals.

Once the bone marrow melts and reaches 190°C/374°F, you can remove the garlic, crispy bits (delicious) and herbs, as they will now have flavoured the bone marrow.

Place a cube of steak onto a metal skewer and dip into the hot melted bone marrow for as long as you like, around 20 seconds is ideal – just long enough to get it crisp outside and blue inside. Season the steak and repeat.

You and your friends can sit and enjoy this dining experience and everyone can have a go. Try other things dipped into the hot bone marrow, too, maybe some cubes of bread or halloumi.

4 marrow bones, cut in half

1 clove garlic

1 small sprig each of rosemary and thyme

800 g/1¾ lb. steak of your choice (I used fillet/tenderloin), cut into 2.5-cm/1-in. cubes

coarse sea salt and freshly ground black pepper

small, deep cast-iron or heavy-duty pan

4 metal skewers

Serves 4

BEEF LINDSTROM BURGERS

I have travelled to various Scandinavian countries with my day job over the years, and while working in Norway I tried Beef Lindstrom, a classic dish from neighbouring Sweden, which is a delicious burger patty with the addition of chopped beetroot/beets and capers. I really wanted to try this on my grill back home.

2 small beetroots/beets

2 tsp capers

240 g/9 oz. minced/ground beef

2 slices toasted sourdough bread

a handful of rocket/arugula

2 tbsp good-quality mayonnaise

1 tsp creamed horseradish

coarse sea salt and freshly ground black pepper

Serves 2

Set up your barbecue for direct cooking over moderate heat (around 180°C/356°F).

Place the beetroots/beets directly in the coals and cook until charred on the outside and soft on the inside, around 25–30 minutes.

Finely chop one of the beetroots/beets and the capers, then add to the beef and mix together. Form the mixture into two patties, then grill over direct heat until the meat is cooked through and has reached an internal temperature of 74°C/165°F.

To serve, top the toasted sourdough bread with the rocket/arugula and then the patties. Mix together the mayonnaise and horseradish and spread on top. Finally, chop the second ember-cooked beetroot and add to the burgers.

KIMCHEESE SAUSAGE RAFTS

One of the most popular recipes from my book Skewered *is the sausage raft, topped with cheese and chimichurri. I fancied trying a Far Eastern version – spicy sausages topped with kimchi and melted Cheddar cheese. The combo was a success, and I was surprised at just how well the flavours worked together.*

5–6 spicy sausages (I went for some firecracker sausages)

3–4 tbsp kimchi

50 g/½ cup grated Cheddar cheese

2 flat metal skewers

Serves 2

Set up your barbecue for lid-on direct cooking at a moderate heat (around 160–180°C/320–356°F).

Place the sausages in a row, nestled side by side. Insert the two skewers through all the sausages, with both skewers about 2 cm/¾ in. from the ends, to secure them together.

Place the skewered sausages on the grill and cook with the barbecue lid down for 8–10 minutes on each side, turning as required so the sausages cook through and don't burn – move them slightly off the direct heat if they are cooking too quickly. You're aiming for an internal temperature of 74°C/165°F.

Spoon over the kimchi and grated Cheddar cheese, then continue to cook with the barbecue lid on for a few minutes until the cheese has melted.

Cut the raft down the middle and serve on the skewers.

CRISPY PORK SHANK TACOS

This is probably one of my favourite recipes out of the ones I've come up with recently. I'm proud of all the recipes I create, but this one is simply spectacular. I've been eating low-carb for a couple of years now, but have missed tacos. By cooking the pork shanks at a high heat, the skin turns into a wonderful crackling, and by taking the meat to 94°C/201°F, you get a juicy pulled pork, which you can then load into the crispy pork-skin 'taco shells'. Heaven.

2 pork shanks, about 1 kg/
2 lb. 4 oz. each

1 large tomato, finely chopped

2 spring onions/scallions, finely chopped

a handful of coriander/cilantro

4 tbsp soured cream

2 tbsp hot sauce of your choice, plus extra to serve

coarse sea salt and freshly ground black pepper

Serves 2

Set up your barbecue for lid-on, two-zone (direct and indirect) cooking at a moderate heat (around 160–180°C/320–356°F). Add a chunk of cherry wood to the coals for a little smoke.

Rub a couple of pinches of salt and pepper into each pork shank.

Place the pork shanks on the barbecue, just to the edge of the direct heat zone, and cook with the lid down until the skin crisps up to a wonderful crackling; around 30–40 minutes.

Once you are happy with the crackling, you need to move the shanks to the indirect heat side to cook slowly with the lid down for 1½ –2 hours until they have an internal temperature of 94°C/201°F. The meat should be tender with little resistance when you insert the temperature probe.

Allow to rest for 20–30 minutes. Meanwhile, mix together the chopped tomato, spring onions/scallions and most of the coriander/cilantro. Season with a pinch of sea salt and black pepper.

Mix together the soured cream and hot sauce.

To serve, carefully cut the crispy pork skin into two pieces to look like taco shells. Pull the pork apart and load into the crispy pork skin taco shells. Top with the spicy cream, a little extra hot sauce and some of the fresh salsa and the remaining coriander/cilantro.

BUFFALO CHICKEN DRUMSTICKS

It's usually chicken wings that get lovingly smothered in piquant buffalo sauce, but a butterflied crispy chicken drumstick covered in homemade buffalo sauce is pretty special, too. Butterflying the drumsticks ensures maximum crispiness.

12 chicken drumsticks

60 g/4 tbsp butter

3–4 tsp hot sauce (I used the traditional Franks)

garlic salt and freshly ground black pepper

soured cream, to serve

finely sliced chilli/chile, to serve

a handful of fresh coriander/ cilantro, to serve

Serves 4

Set up your barbecue for lid-on direct cooking at a moderate heat (around 180–200°C/356–392°F).

Butterfly the chicken drumsticks by running a small sharp knife down one side of the drumstick, right down to the bone, then butterflying out the meat without detaching it from the bone.

Season with plenty of the garlic salt and pepper.

Cook the drumsticks, skin-side down, over direct heat on the barbecue with the lid on until crisping up, about 8–10 minutes. Turn and cook until the chicken is cooked through and has reached an internal temperature of 74°C/165°F.

Make up the buffalo sauce by melting the butter and stirring in the hot sauce.

Smother the drumsticks in the sauce, then serve at once with a drizzle of soured cream and some chilli/chile slices and coriander/cilantro.

Use the handle of the drumstick to hold and prepare to get messy.

CHAPTER 4

BREADS

FENNEL AND HONEY FOCACCIA

I've been doing what I call my Country WoodSmoke Bread (from my first book Food and Fire) for many years now, and it's the main bread I still cook for my family and at my BBQ classes. However, sometimes I like to vary the toppings and this was one I tried that came out so well, I just couldn't stop eating it. Great by itself, or perfect for serving with any of the recipes you can dip bread in.

1 kg/generous 7 cups strong white bread flour

7 g/2¼ tsp active dried yeast

12 g/2 tsp fine salt

4 tbsp extra virgin olive oil

1 fennel bulb, thinly sliced lengthways

1 tbsp runny honey

Serves 8

The night before you want to make the focaccia, put half the flour into a mixing bowl and add the yeast and 650 ml/2¾ cups water. Stir to mix, cover with clingfilm/plastic wrap and leave overnight at room temperature.

The next morning add the rest of the flour and the salt, then, using a stand mixer with a dough hook (it's quite a sticky dough), knead for 10 minutes until silky smooth. Cover the dough and leave in a warm place to rise for 2 hours.

Drizzle half the olive oil into the base of a large baking sheet. Using a dough scraper, transfer the dough into the baking sheet, cover and allow to rise for 1 hour.

Set up your barbecue for lid-on indirect cooking at a high heat (around 220°C/428°F).

Using your fingers dipped into a little olive oil, make some dimples in the top of the dough. Place the slices of fennel bulb on top of the dough and press down lightly. Drizzle over the remaining olive oil.

Bake in the hot barbecue, with the lid on, for 40 minutes until the loaf is golden brown on top and sounds hollow when tapped on the base.

Drizzle over the honey and enjoy warm.

SPICED BUTTER FLATBREAD

I've included flatbreads in previous books, but had never tried to make it with my overnight sponge dough recipe. Grilling the flatbreads over the coals, they puffed up wonderfully and then I brushed them with the spiced melted butter.

500 g/generous 3½ cups strong white bread flour, plus extra for dusting

3 g/1 tsp active dried yeast

6 g/1 tsp fine salt

100 g/7 tbsp salted butter

2 tsp masala spice mix (I used a korma spice mix as my kids like it mild)

2 tsp turmeric powder

Serves 6–8

The night before you want to make the flatbread, put half the flour into a mixing bowl and add the yeast and 325 ml/1⅓ cups water. Stir to mix, cover with clingfilm/plastic wrap and leave overnight at room temperature.

The next morning add the rest of the flour and the salt, then, using a stand mixer with a dough hook (it's quite a sticky dough), knead for 10 minutes until silky smooth. Cover the dough and leave in a warm place to rise for 2 hours.

Knock back/punch down the dough, then, on a lightly floured surface, divide the dough into 100–150-g/3½–5¼-oz. portions and roll them into balls. Cover and allow to rise for 1 hour.

Set up your barbecue for direct cooking at a high heat (around 200°C/392°F).

Using a little flour on a board, stretch a ball of dough out until it's quite thin, then place it directly over the hot coals. Cook for a couple of minutes, then turn it before it burns and cook for a couple of minutes on the other side. The dough should puff and bubble. Repeat with the remaining dough.

Melt the butter in a pan and stir in the spices, brush onto each flatbread and serve.

CHORIZO ROLLS

I spent many happy days enjoying the most delicious chorizo rolls while in Portugal for a month when I was at university studying the local geology. These rolls are stuffed with chorizo, which oozes delicious russet-coloured juices into the surrounding bread, and the resulting taste is one that you'll never forget.

500 g/generous 3½ cups strong white bread flour, plus extra for dusting

3 g/1 tsp active dried yeast

6 g/1 tsp fine salt

4 cooking chorizo sausages

Serves 4

The night before you want to make the rolls, put half the flour into a mixing bowl and add the yeast and 325 ml/1⅓ cups water. Stir to mix, cover with clingfilm/plastic wrap and leave overnight at room temperature.

The next morning add the rest of the flour and the salt, then, using a stand mixer with a dough hook (it's quite a sticky dough), knead for 10 minutes until silky smooth. Cover the dough and leave in a warm place to rise for 2 hours.

Knock back/punch down the dough, then, on a lightly floured surface, divide the dough into four portions (200 g/7 oz. each) and roll them into sausage shapes.

Cut the cooking chorizo sausages in half lengthways and remove the skins. Press both halves of each chorizo into the centre of a dough portion and shape the dough around the chorizo to enclose it completely. Place on a baking sheet, cover and allow to rise for 1 hour.

Set up your barbecue for indirect, lid-on cooking at a high heat (around 200°C/392°F).

Make three slashes along the top of each roll and bake in the hot barbecue over indirect heat, with the barbecue lid on, for around 25–30 minutes until the rolls are cooked through.

CHEESY DUTCH OVEN DAMPER BREAD

This is a simple damper bread recipe, which you can bring together really quickly if you don't have any bread in the house. It's great dipped into saucy recipes, soups and stews. It resembles a large cheese scone and is best served warm. The cheese topping really makes it.

450 g/scant 3½ cups self-raising/self-rising flour, plus extra for dusting

2 tsp sea salt

1 tbsp caster/superfine sugar

35 g/2½ tbsp softened butter, plus extra to serve

60 g/⅔ cup grated mature/sharp Cheddar cheese

cast-iron Dutch oven or heavy-duty pan with a lid, lined with parchment or foil

Serves 4

Set up your barbecue for lid-on indirect cooking at a high heat (around 200°C/392°F).

In a bowl, stir together the flour, salt and sugar, then add the softened butter and crumble it into the flour with your fingers. Add 300 ml/1¼ cups water and knead together until relatively smooth; around 5–6 minutes.

Dust a little flour onto the base of the lined Dutch oven or pan and pour in your bread mix.

With a sharp knife, make a cross on the top of the loaf, cutting down quite deep. Sprinkle over the grated cheese. Cover with the lid.

Bake on the hot barbecue, with the barbecue lid on, for 25 minutes, then remove the pan lid and cook for another 20–25 minutes until the cheese and the top of the bread is brown.

Serve warm with plenty of butter.

'NDUJA GARLIC BUTTER BREAD

This is a simple and delicious spicy version of cheesy garlic bread. You may well have noticed I'm a little bit obsessed with 'nduja. This spicy spreadable salami just melts into little puddles of fatty heaven when heated and is perfect on cheesy garlic bread to give it a little kick. I always use Duchy Charcuterie 'nduja, which is the best I've tasted.

500 g/generous 3½ cups strong white bread flour, plus extra for dusting

3 g/1 tsp active dried yeast

6 g/1 tsp fine salt

2 tbsp 'nduja

2 cloves garlic, finely chopped

30 g/2 tbsp softened butter

4 handfuls of grated Cheddar or mozzarella cheese

pizza stone

Serves 4

The night before you want to make the bread, put half the flour into a mixing bowl and add the yeast and 325 ml/1⅓ cups water. Stir to mix, cover with clingfilm/plastic wrap and leave overnight at room temperature.

The next morning add the rest of the flour and the salt, then, using a stand mixer with a dough hook (it's quite a sticky dough), knead for 10 minutes until silky smooth. Cover the dough and leave in a warm place to rise for 2 hours.

Divide the dough into four balls and dust with flour.

Set up your barbecue with a pizza stone for lid-on cooking at a high heat (around 220°C/428°F).

Flatten out the dough balls to 5 mm–1 cm/¼–⅛ in. thick disks, then bake on the pizza stone for 15 minutes with the barbecue lid on, turning if the base gets too dark.

Mix together the 'nduja, garlic and butter, and spread one-quarter over each bread, then top with a handful of cheese. Place back into the heat to melt the cheese for a few minutes. Repeat with the remaining dough and toppings.

Slice and get stuck in.

SMOKED GARLIC AND THYME LOAF

This recipe uses my favourite overnight sponge method, as most of the bread recipes here do. I've found it works for loaves, rolls, pizzas and flatbreads. Here I've pepped up the base recipe to make a tasty loaf with some smoked garlic and thyme.

1 kg/generous 7 cups strong white bread flour

7 g/2¼ tsp active dried yeast

12g/2 tsp fine salt

3 cloves hot smoked garlic, finely chopped

2 tbsp thyme leaves

8–10 sprigs of thyme

Serves 4-6

The night before you want to make the loaf, put half the flour into a mixing bowl and add the yeast and 650 ml/2¾ cups water. Stir to mix, cover with clingfilm/plastic wrap and leave overnight at room temperature.

The next morning add the rest of the flour and the salt, then, using a stand mixer with a dough hook (it's quite a sticky dough), knead for 10 minutes until silky smooth. Cover the dough and leave in a warm place to rise for 2 hours.

Knock back/punch down the dough, then add the finely chopped smoked garlic and thyme leaves and form into a round loaf shape. Place on a baking sheet, cover and allow to rise for 1 hour.

Set up your barbecue for lid-on indirect cooking at a high heat (around 200°C/392°F).

Slash the top of the loaf with a sharp knife and top the loaf with the thyme sprigs.

Bake in the hot barbecue over indirect heat with the lid on (add a splash of water in a metal bowl for a bit of steam to help the crust), for around 40 minutes until the bread sounds hollow when you tap the base.

Allow to cool before slicing and serving.

CHAPTER 5

CONDIMENTS

SMOKY CHILLI/CHILI OIL

Adding a hint of smoke to an oil adds a lick of extra flavour to all sorts of food. I always find it a useful thing to have handy; I add to salads and grilled veg, and it's just wonderful drizzled over pizza. You could try dipping bread in it, such as the Fennel and Honey Focaccia on page 139. The process is quite simple, and you can choose the wood embers, or just use charcoal, to vary the flavours the oil takes on. The chilli flakes/hot red pepper flakes just give a wonderful colour and a bit of heat, so choose your chilli/chile variety wisely.

Place the olive oil and chilli flakes/hot red pepper flakes into a heat-resistant bowl.

Take an ember of hardwood, fruitwood or lumpwood charcoal – I went for a sweet smoky chunk of cherry ember – and carefully place it in the oil. It should start to smoke.

Cover the bowl snugly with a sheet of foil and leave for about 10 minutes; the foil will trap the smoke, which infuses into the oil.

Have a taste of the oil, and repeat if you want a smokier flavour. Leave to mellow overnight in a covered bowl.

Store covered in the fridge for up to 1 week.

100 ml/⅓ cup light olive oil

2 tsp Aleppo chilli flakes/hot red pepper flakes

Makes 110 ml/ scant ½ cup

CHARRED HERB OIL

Fats, oils and salts are great carriers of flavour, and toasted herbs are particularly wonderful flavours to carry onto your meats, fish or vegetables. You can use any combination of woody herbs, such as rosemary, thyme or bay.

a few sprigs of woody herbs, such as rosemary, thyme or bay

2 tsp coarse sea salt

100 ml/⅓ cup olive oil

Makes 125 ml/½ cup

Place the herbs and salt into a heat-resistant bowl and then carefully place a lump of hot lumpwood charcoal or a hardwood/fruitwood ember on top of the herbs. They should release a fragrant smoke and go slightly charred and crispy after a few minutes.

Remove the charcoal and use a mortar and pestle to crunch up the herbs and salt. Add the olive oil and leave to infuse for 2 hours.

You can leave the herbs in or strain them out. Store covered in the fridge for up to 1 week.

SMOKED OIL VINAIGRETTE

It may seem strange to include a vinaigrette in a book about barbecue, but, for me, you can add barbecue flavours to a whole host of dishes, even a simple salad. The addition of something smoky or charred adds such a wonderful depth of flavour. You have an option here of using some of the Charred Herb Oil on page 153, or the Smoky Chilli/Chili Oil on page 152 as the base for your salad dressing.

100 ml/⅓ cup Charred Herb Oil (see page 153) or Smoky Chilli/Chili Oil (see page 152)

2 tsp red wine vinegar

1 tsp Dijon or mild mustard

coarse sea salt or smoked salt

Serves 4–6

Add all of the ingredients into a jug/pitcher with a good pinch of salt and whisk together.

Use to dress a wonderful selection of salads or grilled veg.

Store covered in the fridge for up to 1 week.

TOASTED HERB MAYONNAISE

A good mayonnaise recipe is a wonderful thing to have in your barbecue repertoire. It can lift any number of grilled veg, fish or meat dishes. I like to add an extra element to my mayonnaise by using the whole egg and charred woody herbs.

6–8 sprigs of rosemary or thyme (or a combination of both)

1 UK large/US extra-large egg

240 ml/1 cup light olive oil

1 tbsp freshly squeezed lemon juice

sea salt

heatproof mortar and pestle

Serves 4

Place the herbs in a heatproof mortar and toast the herbs with a blow torch or a chunk of hot charcoal. Then use the pestle to grind the herbs to a fine powder.

In a tall narrow jug/pitcher, place the egg, oil, lemon juice and a pinch of salt. Using a stick blender, blitz until it forms a thick and creamy mayonnaise. Pour the mayonnaise into the mortar and stir to combine the toasted herbs.

Store covered in the fridge for up to 2 days.

CHIMICHURRI ROJO BUTTER

You may well have noticed that I love chimichurri, and it can come in many different variations. One of my favourites is the slightly sweeter chimichurri rojo (red chimichurri). I use a charred sweet red mini (bell) pepper to add that wonderful sweetness. It's great as a condiment in itself, but here I mix it with butter. Perfect to add an extra depth of flavour to the Smoked and Braised Oxtail on page 100.

1 sweet red mini (bell) pepper

2 cloves garlic

2 good pinches coarse sea salt

80 ml/⅓ cup extra virgin olive oil

2 tsp red wine vinegar

2 tbsp dried oregano

2 tbsp Aleppo chilli flakes/ hot red pepper flakes

a small handful of fresh oregano or marjoram

a good handful of fresh flat-leaf parsley

200 g/1¾ stick softened butter

Makes 340 g/1¹/₂ cups

Set up your barbecue for direct cooking at a moderate heat (around 160°C/320°F).

Char the sweet mini red (bell) pepper directly over the coals for a few minutes to char slightly and soften. Remove the stem and core/seeds.

Place the pepper in a jug/pitcher with all the remaining ingredients except the butter, and blitz up with a stick blender to a coarse paste.

Mix the chimichurri with the softened butter, then wrap in clingfilm/ plastic wrap to make a sausage shape and place in the fridge to set.

To use, cut circles of the chimichurri rojo butter and add to grilled vegetables, fish or meats.

Store wrapped in the fridge for up to 2 days.

MAPLE CHILLI/CHILI BUTTER

A simple way to pep up the flavour of grilled veg, a plump crispy pork chop or even popcorn. Just add a little to your hot food and watch it melt...

60 g/4 tbsp softened butter

2 tsp maple syrup

2 tsp Aleppo chilli flakes/hot red pepper flakes

Makes 75 g/5 tbsp

Mix all the ingredients together thoroughly in a bowl.

Cover and keep in the fridge for as long as you can resist.

CHARRED HERB SALT

This is something I've been playing with for a while now. You create a wonderfully fragrant salt that can be used to pep up all kinds of dishes, depending on the herbs you use. Woody herbs are the best (bay, thyme and rosemary) either on their own or in combination. Have a play!

Place the salt in the stone mortar or cast-iron pan. Place the herbs on top.

Place a piece of hot, glowing lumpwood charcoal or a hardwood/fruitwood ember on top of the herbs and salt for 10–20 seconds; just enough to toast the herbs without totally charring them.

Either crush up the salt and charred herbs using a pestle or blitz them in a spice grinder, removing any woody stalks.

Store covered for up to 1 week.

4 tbsp good-quality coarse sea salt

a couple of bay leaves or a couple of sprigs of rosemary or thyme

stone mortar and pestle or cast-iron pan

Makes 4 tbsp

CHAPTER 6

SWEET THINGS
AND DRINKS

RHUBARB CRUMBLE AND CUSTARD PIZZA

At the end of a wood-fired pizza session, we often have a ball or two of dough left, and my kids love to get creative with sweet pizza recipes. These often involve chocolate hazelnut spread, but sometimes we try something else, and this recipe came out of one of these experiments. The custard works so well with the sharp rhubarb and crunchy granola. The pizza dough recipe here makes 8 balls.

1 ball pizza dough (see below)

4 tbsp store-bought custard/ vanilla custard sauce

a handful of finely sliced pink rhubarb

3 tbsp granola

PIZZA DOUGH *(makes 8 balls)*

1 kg/generous 7 cups strong white bread flour, plus extra for dusting

650 ml/2¾ cups water

7 g/2¼ tsp active dried yeast

12 g/2½ tsp fine sea salt

pizza stone

Serves 2–4

Start your pizza dough the night before. Mix half of the flour with the water and yeast. Stir to combine, cover and leave overnight.

About 3 hours before you plan to make pizza, add the rest of the flour and the salt, and knead for 10 minutes in a food processor with a dough hook or by hand. Cover the bowl and allow to prove for 1 hour in a warm place.

Using a dough scraper, scrape out the dough onto a floured surface and split into 8 equal balls. Roll the balls until smooth. Cover and allow to rest for an hour.

Set up your barbecue with a pizza stone and heat to as hot as you can get it, or heat a wood-fired oven to 350–400°C/662–752°F.

Roll out one of the dough balls to make your pizza base. Spoon over the custard and spread it evenly over the pizza base, leaving a little gap at the edge of the dough. Sprinkle over the rhubarb slices and granola.

Transfer to the hot pizza stone or into the pizza oven and cook until the pizza edge is crispy, 2–4 minutes depending on the temperature.

MARSHMALLOW DIPPING CONES

My kids (of course!) came up with this recipe at the end of a barbecue meal. It's a fun twist on toasted marshmallows dipped in chocolate. Always a winner.

Prepare your barbecue with a small amount of lit coals. You can also use a firepit.

Place the pan close to the heat but not directly over the coals. Add the chocolate buttons to the pan and allow to melt.

Push the skewers through the base of the cones, then push the marshmallows onto the end of the skewer at the top of the cone.

Hold the marshmallow over the coals to warm and go soft for a few minutes – you don't want it too soft, but toast it enough to get a little bit of caramelization on the marshmallow.

Dip the marshmallows into the melted chocolate, then pull the skewer back out of the cone (careful, it might be hot). Wait for the chocolate and marshmallow to cool a little, then get stuck in.

2 ice cream cones

2 giant barbecue toasting marshmallows

100 g/3½ oz. milk or dark/bittersweet chocolate buttons

small heavy-duty pan

2 long wooden skewers, soaked in water

Serves 2

BISCOFF S'MORE ROLLS

Unsurprisingly, this is a recipe my kids came up with, and it has become a firm (very sweet) family favourite! It is a riff on the chocolate hazelnut brioche rolls in my Food and Fire *book. It's great to get the kids involved in fire cooking with adult help – with a bit of guidance they will soon feel confident in a skill that will stay with them for life (and there's nothing wrong with a bit of sweet fun at the end of a barbecue meal).*

Set up your barbecue for direct cooking at low–moderate heat (around 140–160°C/284–320°F). You can also use a firepit.

Place a marshmallow on each skewer (these should be long enough to keep little hands away from the heat) and let the kids toast them slowly over the coals until they are soft and lightly browned on the outside.

Toast the brioche buns lightly directly on or over the coals.

Spread 1 tbsp Biscoff Spread onto the base of each brioche roll.

Place the toasted marshmallow on top of the Biscoff Spread, add the top of the roll and, using the roll to keep the marshmallow in place, withdraw the skewer.

Wrap the whole roll in foil (to keep in the melting Biscoff Spread) and place near the coals to warm up for 4–5 minutes.

Enjoy! It's messy, but delicious.

2 brioche rolls

2 giant barbecue marshmallows

2 tbsp Lotus Biscoff (Speculoos spiced cookie spread)

2 long, flat metal skewers

Serves 2

SMOKED APRICOT AND BOURBON

I worked this recipe up when I was working at a barbecue show. The sponsor was a great bourbon brand and I needed to come up with a smoky cocktail using the bourbon, so I smoked some apricots, blitzed them up and added bourbon – and found it was a winner.

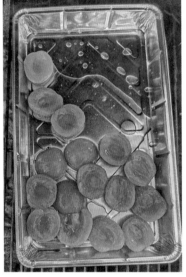

Set up your barbecue for lid-on indirect cooking at a low heat (around 100–120°C/212–248°F), with a chunk of cherry or apple wood on the coals for smoke.

Place the apricots onto a baking sheet and cook in your barbecue over indirect heat for around an hour to smoke with the lid on.

Remove the apricots and allow to cool.

Blitz the apricot halves in a food processor or blender to a purée.

Put a handful of crushed ice into two tall glasses. Add 2–3 tbsp smoked apricot purée to each glass and top up with a couple of shots of bourbon. Stir and serve.

400-g/14-oz. can apricot halves in light syrup, drained

100 ml/⅓ cup/4 shots bourbon

a couple of handfuls of crushed ice

Serves 2

GRILLED RHUBARB GIN FIZZ

A deliciously refreshing cocktail with a smoky caramelized twist. A rhubarb gin fizz is a refreshing, slightly sharp cocktail, but grilling the rhubarb adds a surprising twist.

Set up your barbecue for direct cooking at a moderate heat (160°C/320°F).

Grill the rhubarb pieces over direct heat for 6–8 minutes until lightly golden and softened. Allow to cool.

Add the sugar, gin and rhubarb to a bowl. Use a stick blender to purée, then strain through a fine sieve/strainer, using the back of a spoon to push the mixture through and remove any stringy bits.

Put the ice into two glasses and then add half of the purée to each glass. Top up with the sparkling wine and serve.

1 stick pink rhubarb, cut into 8-cm/3¼-in. pieces

2 tsp caster/superfine sugar

100 ml/⅓ cup/4 shots gin

300 ml/1¼ cups sparkling wine (I used a pink prosecco)

a couple of handfuls of crushed ice

Serves 2

BUFFALO BLOOD COCKTAIL

This is barely a cocktail, but is a delicious way to enjoy a longer bourbon and makes a change from cola. The beetroot/beet juice gives a delicious earthy sweetness that goes well with bourbon. Try it, you might be surprised.

a handful of ice cubes

50 ml/3½ tbsp beetroot/beet juice

50 ml/3½ tbsp/2 shots bourbon

Serves 1

Simply add the ice to a glass (I went for an old fashioned glass) and pour in the beetroot/beet juice and bourbon.

Stir and serve.

INDEX

ACKNOWLEDGMENTS

My family are my world, and my wife Lisa is always supporting, sharing our journey through life's up and downs. I could not do any of this without you.

Rory, Elsie and Louie are my chief tasting team, if a recipe doesn't get past them it doesn't get in the book, they also help me to remember that BBQ should be fun.

Dad you are my hero, and Mum I miss you.

To all my dear friends and family, it's been a tough couple of years, but thank you for your love, support and guidance. Let's hope we can spend more time together sat around the firepit.

BBQ family are simply the best, we've grown in numbers considerably in the last couple of years, due to us all wanting to share our love of good food cooked outdoors.

Those who have attended classes at my UK BBQ School in Devon, thank you for coming to me for guidance and inspiration, I love to teach BBQ, and sharing with you, helps me to keep my own fires burning.

Thank you to my Agent Robert Gwyn Palmer for your unwavering belief in me – it's always a lift when we have a catch-up chat.

Thank you to all at Ryland Peters & Small team for helping to bring this book to life – Julia, Sally, Geoff, Kate and team – you have helped me bring my literary dreams to fruition, thank you so much.

To all the businesses I work with who support what I do at CountryWoodSmoke – all the Butchers, BBQ companies, charcoal makers, rub and sauce producers, and to the retailers who are stocking this book. Thank you to the team at Meater® thermometers, it's been great working with you all over the years –it's an exciting time for UK BBQ and I am enjoying sharing the ride with you. Thank you to Tom, James and the team at Fordmore Farm Shop for all your support.

Thank you to the BBQ Mag team, you've taken a digital dream of a BBQ Magazine and turned it into something epic, that is continuing to evolve, grow and inspire our readers.

Thank you to Matt Fowler for all the photography and video work. We've worked through some good, and some not-so-easy times.

Everyone at the Guild of Food Writers, you continue to inspire, support and put up with my dirty bbq pictures.